Financial Aid through Social Work

Financial Aid through Social Work (1979) examines the way in which financial aid through social work has been used and the consequences of such use. Beginning with an examination of the historical and comparative background, the book looks at the decisions made by social workers on financial aid and the way in which they are arrived at. Among the questions examined are the extent to which there is any well-defined policy on financial aid, the overlap between the work of social work departments and other agencies, and the effect that financial aid has on the relationship between clients and social workers.

Financial Aid through Social Work

Michael P. Jackson and B. Michael Valencia

Routledge
Taylor & Francis Group

First published in 1979
by Routledge & Kegan Paul Ltd

This edition first published in 2025 by Routledge
4 Park Square, Milton Park, Abingdon, Oxon, OX14 4RN

and by Routledge
605 Third Avenue, New York, NY 10017

Routledge is an imprint of the Taylor & Francis Group, an informa business

© 1979 Michael P. Jackson and B. Michael Valencia

Publisher's Note
The publisher has gone to great lengths to ensure the quality of this reprint but points out that some imperfections in the original copies may be apparent.

Disclaimer
The publisher has made every effort to trace copyright holders and welcomes correspondence from those they have been unable to contact.

A Library of Congress record exists under LCCN 78041330

ISBN: 978-1-032-93351-1 (hbk)
ISBN: 978-1-003-56557-4 (ebk)
ISBN: 978-1-032-93365-8 (pbk)

Book DOI 10.4324/9781003565574

Financial aid through social work

Michael P. Jackson and B. Michael Valencia
Department of Sociology University of Stirling

Routledge & Kegan Paul
London, Boston and Henley

First published in 1979
by Routledge & Kegan Paul Ltd
39 Store Street, London WC1E 7DD,
Broadway House, Newtown Road,
Henley-on-Thames, Oxon RG9 1EN and
9 Park Street, Boston, Mass. 02108, USA
Set in 10 on 11pt English
and printed in Great Britain by
The Lavenham Press Limited
Lavenham, Suffolk

British Library Cataloguing in Publication Data

Jackson, Michael Peart
Financial aid through social work—(Library of social work:
0305-4381).
1 Social service—Great Britain
2 Economic assistance, Domestic—Great Britain
I Title II Valencia, B Michael
361'.05'0941   HV245   78-41330

ISBN 0 7100 0176 2

Contents

Tables

Acknowledgments

We have been involved in research concerning financial aid through social work for a number of years. We have been helped by a variety of people and organizations: a number of Scottish social work departments, social workers, clients and local authority councillors. The bulk of our work has been funded by the Social Work Services Group (Scottish Education Department) although in the early stages finance was also provided by the Nuffield Foundation. It is clear that our research would not have been possible without the help we have been given.

It is also clear to us how important it is in research like this to receive the encouragement and support of colleagues. We are particularly grateful for the encouragement given by Dr G. Smith, Ms J. Aimes and Mr J. Tibbett (all at times of the Social Work Services Group), Professor D. Timms, and Professor C. Turner (Department of Sociology, Stirling).

A number of people have been employed as research staff on the project and we have been fortunate to enjoy the services of two excellent secretaries, Mrs C. Wordley and Mrs C. Gregory. We have also been assisted by another lecturer in the Department of Sociology at Stirling, Mr Richard Bland. He has contributed especially to the work reported in chapters 3 and 6 of the book.

A number of people have commented on drafts of this book. We are particularly indebted to Mr John Tibbett and to Professor Noel Timms. Professor Timms as editor of the series was a constant source of advice and encouragement.

Introduction

Integrated social work departments were established in England and Wales in 1971[1] and in Scotland in 1969[2]. Reorganization was the culmination of years of agitation and discussion[3]. It was anticipated that the new structure would permit a better (more co-ordinated) service to be offered to clients and would encourage the development of a unified social work profession[4]. Although there are few comprehensive evaluations of the new structure[5] (arguably it is too early to undertake such a task effectively) there is wide agreement that a variety of problems still exist.

Some of these problems may be the result of the exaggerated expectations that preceded and accompanied reorganization. Senior members of the new departments sometimes encouraged in their communities expectations of a comprehensive service that were never likely to be fulfilled. The subsequent economic stringencies made fulfilment practically impossible. Disappointment and confusion resulted not only for clients but also for social workers and persons working closely with the new departments, like doctors, teachers and nurses.

It is also arguable that reorganization has not resulted in the enhancement of the 'social work role' that some expected. Social workers, themselves, are often confused by the tasks they are asked to perform: people who joined departments wanting to be 'social workers' find themselves assessing applicants for various services rationed out by local authorities, escorting children to holidays, collecting weekly payments for other agencies and even issuing concessionary bus tickets to retired people. To many these duties seem inappropriate if not undignified. Some writers have argued that abandoning formal specialization has led to less rather than more precisely defined roles for social workers. Butrym suggests that before the establishment of integrated departments, most workers in the social services had succeeded to some degree in distinguishing between work which required their intervention and that which could be carried out by non social work staff or volunteers[6]. This was most true in 'settings' such as children's departments and medical social work, which not only had relatively high proportions of qualified staff but also had a clear understanding of 'agency function',[7] which was then a notion of central importance for social casework defining in general, but quite clear terms, the tasks which each department was set up to perform and providing staff with quite clear ideas about the proper role of the social worker. Since 1971, the new pressures and uncertainties in integrated departments mean that 'agency function' is now of little help in describing social work in local authorities.

In Scotland the confusion is aggravated, for there personal social services were integrated in 1969 into departments of social *work* rather than social service. It may be that the nomenclature itself adds to confusion about the specifically social work function. Unlike their English and Welsh counterparts, they are responsible for probation, prison welfare and parole services, and the legislation under which they operate is far wider, for unlike the social service departments elsewhere, they are governed by a general direction to 'promote welfare'. Another difficulty, north of the border, is that despite a major reorganization in 1975, social work departments have not yet settled effectively into an appropriate administrative structure.

While the confusion over the social work task causes problems and embarrassment for social workers, its effect is by no means confined to them. Clients may no longer be shunted from one local authority department to another when seeking help but they may now credit the social service or social work department with a function far wider than its remit. The personnel of other agencies, like the Supplementary Benefits Commission, or local authority housing departments might have expectations which social workers are unable or unwilling to fulfil and this may result in personal and organizational conflict.

Reorganization may not have caused other problems but it may have failed to provide a solution for them. For example, many social workers are still perplexed about the function of their profession in society. They are uncertain how to answer the criticism that their activities do little to further the long term 'good' of their clients, that they are doing little more than providing short term palliatives. Similarly, many social workers are concerned that the path to advancement is into posts demanding management ability, but with little contact with clients of the service. Reorganization, by creating larger units, may have exacerbated this problem.

All this is not to suggest that reorganization has been without benefits, nor that on balance its benefits may not outweigh its disadvantages. Anyway this is not the place to attempt such judgments. We have not sought to denigrate social work as an activity or social workers as praçtitioners. Our aim, rather, has been to highlight some of the problems and conflicts inherent in modern social work so as to provide a background for our main discussion of the role of financial aid in social work.

Since 1963 social work departments in Britain have had the power, in certain circumstances, to give financial aid to clients directly. In other countries, too, social workers have been responsible for the distribution of financial assistance. These powers have raised a number of crucial issues and problems. For example, should money be associated with social work at all and what part should qualified social workers play in its distribution? What scope should there be for independent discretion by social workers? What are the demands which other services could legitimately make on the social work services? What are the expectations of the client public? What effect does the power to give financial aid have on the client/social worker relationship?

The importance of such questions can only be appreciated when viewed against the background of developments and uncertainty in social work more generally. Such uncertainties have exacerbated the problems over financial aid. However, at the same time the problems over financial aid mirror many of the general uncertainties and bring them sharply into focus.

We shall concentrate on three major themes. First, we shall examine the ways in which the financial aid responsibilities of social work departments overlap with similar responsibilities in other agencies. Second, we shall look at the way social workers make decisions on financial aid and at some of the factors that influence these decisions. Third, we shall speculate about the consequences of the decision made, for example, on the relationship of financial aid to the social work task.

Most of the discussion will be based on British material. We will look at the history of legislation on financial aid through social work in Britain and at the way powers to give financial aid have been used. We will also look at the relationship between social service and social work departments and bodies like the Supplementary Benefits Commission, housing departments and fuel authorities. We will then present an analysis of the way decisions are made on financial aid in Britain. However we will also examine what major social work writers have had to say on financial aid (this necessarily demands a look in particular at American literature) and at international experience.

Chapter one

Britain: post Second World War experience

It can be argued that a discussion of the relationship between social work and financial aid needs to take account of developments in Britain as far back as the nineteenth century. However, the social legislation of the 1940s is a useful starting point for a discussion of recent developments, for it marked the beginning of social work within local authorities in Britain and the establishment of a comprehensive income maintenance service. It also marked the attempt to impose a strict barrier between income maintenance and social work services. For the next fifteen years or so, in organizational terms at least, state financial aid and social work were firmly separated.

Income maintenance and social work provisions after the Second World War

Prior to the Second World War social insurance schemes were patchy and far from comprehensive, while the Poor Law administered by local authorities provided public assistance. After the Second World War, National Insurance schemes were extended and re-organized to cover the entire working population and a National Assistance scheme established to ensure a subsistence income for anyone who 'fell through the net' of the contributory schemes. These were expected to provide an adequate subsistence income to all who were without work or sufficient private means. The abolition of the Poor Law in 1948 was intended to take away from local authorities all responsibility for relief, except for residential services for elderly and handicapped people who because of their infirmities, rather than lack of means, could not live comfortably outside residential institutions and for temporary accommodation for people in urgent need arising from circumstances (such as fire and flood) which could not have been foreseen.

There was no provision for any form of personal welfare service within the national income maintenance services, even National Assistance.[1] The dominant belief of the immediate postwar period was that financial need arose not from personal improvidence but from the inefficiency of the economic processes of society which failed to provide incomes for all through the labour market. Thus dependence on the insurance and assistance schemes was assumed to arise from the malfunctioning of society rather than the dependent person's inability to manage his affairs or his general delinquency. The recipient of assistance was to be free to manage his income without guidance or supervision, and there was no expectation that, basic income needs having been met, he might have more personal difficulties requiring public attention than any other member of society.

The ethos of the time was a crude 'universalism'. Contemporaries found it difficult to reconcile the idea of these broad state services with anything but standard benefits for all persons eligible by a common test of need. Though in the regulations governing the assistance scheme, additions to cover unusual needs such as special diets, heating needs and heavy laundry requirements were permitted, this discretionary element received little consideration at the beginning of the scheme.[2] Little thought was given, either, to the fact that assistance was not available to anyone in full time employment however low his income and however unusual his family's needs.[3]

It was thought that in the main exceptional needs would be met not by the state services but by voluntary organizations. Thus, Lord Beveridge, architect of the insurance and assistance schemes, stated that:[4]

> Whatever the state does, since that must be the same for all
> citizens, there will always remain the scope for personal help
> and individual care of those who need something more or
> different. There will always remain the need for a Society such
> as yours to make charity constructive and healing.

Interestingly, voluntary organizations often combined financial aid with family casework.

But the voluntary societies could not go far to meet the total of such needs. They covered the country only patchily and several family agencies such as the Family Welfare Association adapted to the new social service structure and modern ideas of casework by deliberately accepting fewer clients in order to do more intensive work.[5]

The philosophy of the statutory personal social services, which developed after 1948, complemented that of income maintenance. It was not considered that a general class of persons might exist who

5

might have a need for general social work and there was little appreciation that the needs of potential clients might not fit easily into a number of separate categories defined in a limited number of statutes. 'In the "welfare state" the roads to ruin would at last be blocked.'[6] Thus, the Children's Act 1948 provided for children who needed care outside their own homes; the National Assistance Act (Part III) gave responsibilities to local authorities concerning the elderly and the handicapped and the National Health Service Act required local authorities to give 'advice on the care of young children, persons suffering from illness and expectant or nursing mothers'. The Education Act 1944 and the Criminal Justice Act 1948 consolidated legislation concerning welfare services for children and the probation of offenders respectively.

Each of these services was provided by a separate department of the local authority and each developed its own occupational group gaining its own experience of its specialized clientele and developing professional aspirations relating to its area of work. Thus, it quickly became clear that the staff of the children's departments, variously titled child care officers, boarding out officers and child welfare officers, had more than the quasi-administrative function of receiving children into care. In order to carry out their statutory duties, they had to find and inspect foster homes and communicate between the children's home, the foster home and the child's own family.[7] Similarly, health visitors, whose training was in nursing and health education, were in some places given tasks with the aged and mentally handicapped, while mental welfare officers, many of whom were without formal training, expanded their duties from those concerned with compulsory admission to hospital to general support work in cases of mental handicap and mental illness in the community.[8]

With minor exceptions these specialized services were without powers to give financial aid to their clients.[9] In retrospect, we know that these new social workers must often have encountered financial need in their work. Although the prevailing wisdom suggested that poverty had been virtually eliminated, the low level of income maintenance benefits, which were based on pre war measures of poverty, not the increasing living standards of the 1950s, meant that financial need remained widespread. In addition, the lack of any form of income support, apart from small family allowances, for the low wage earner, meant that caseworkers from the various departments encountered clients who besides their other difficulties had money problems.[10]

The extent to which social workers took notice of these money problems and the steps they took to help their clients with them is difficult to estimate. In so far as many workers had no special training and their instructions related only to defined sets of duties, such as to arrange for children's reception into care, some may have disregarded acute needs which might not have been seen as related to the tasks they had been set. Many accepted the conventional wisdom of the elimination of poverty and failed to see their clients' financial problems. It would be wrong, however, to charge that generation of social workers with blindness to the facts or with failure to search for resources which would help their clients in difficulty. Some had resources in their own control, such as charitable funds administered by local authorities,[11] and many spent a great deal of time applying to voluntary bodies on behalf of their clients. Some found themselves taking up cases with the National Assistance Board regularly and the relationship and boundary issues between social work and the assistance service, which are now a matter of wide concern, began to arise at that time. For people eligible for help from the National Assistance Board, there was an advantage in being aware of the discretionary allowances which could be claimed. The number of discretionary additions to scale rates made by the National Assistance Board increased from 341,000 in 1948 to 1,117,000 in 1956.[12] The claimant trying to live on a comparatively low assistance income who knew which of his needs might get special consideration from the Board stood at an advantage. As the personal social services developed some social workers took up clients' cases with the Board's local offices and began to see this as part of the day to day activity of social work.

The problem family and preventive social work

Financial problems usually presented themselves to social workers in one or more of the following ways: the client might need items necessary for basic hygiene or comfort and yet have no resources to obtain them; there might be a debt which if not paid immediately would result in dire consequences such as eviction, or the social worker might be aware of a debt or need which seemed likely to swamp the client in the foreseeable future. Yet in the immediate post-war years, social workers possessed no general explanation of why these problems occurred or of what their official responsibilities as social workers were in helping their clients to deal with them. If a spell of sickness had left a family with debts, the social worker might be sympathetic with the client's bad luck, or more harshly point to evidence of improvidence, such as hire purchase commitments. 'Many families have taken the opportunity of high wages to make heavy HP commitments', a social worker told Jeffreys, '—something which didn't happen years ago. So when the wage isn't coming in they're in severe financial straits even with improved national insurance benefits.'[13]

But if social workers found only conventional explanations for what they saw, many were sympathetic people in contact with distress, and they looked for ways in which their organizations could help people in obvious difficulties beyond applying the meagre cash resources which they might be able to call on. They wanted guidance on how they should act as social workers. Those who participated in the professional communities of child care officers, probation officers and the like looked for some way in which social policy could accommodate to the problems of financial need which they found in their work. The type of policy which they sought would be one which would give social workers in local government a role which was consistent with their development as professional groups with expert knowledge and skills.

Psychoanalytic theory provided the inspiration for an explanation of individual poverty attributing it in large part to the client's self-destructive and antisocial actions. The client's situation was largely the result of his own behaviour, which was directed by forces within himself of which he was largely unaware.[14] The version of this approach put to use in social work usually included a strong appreciation of the client's present circumstances and the client's reactions to existing pressures such as his marital relationship as well as to his early experiences.[15] The social worker's task was to help him to perceive and overcome the interpersonal difficulties which generally accounted for his material problems.

The most influential presentation of this theory was the model of the 'problem family'. This was adopted particularly by the child care service, but was also much used by other workers, such as health visitors, who were perplexed by families which, despite full employment and the social services, presented problems of material needs.

The idea of the 'slum family' in which material need is associated with antisocial behaviour is a long tradition in British social thinking.[16] What was novel about problem families was that they were perceived as isolated units characterized by atavistic, irresponsible behaviour and multiple difficulties which exasperated the social services. They usually lived amongst non problem neighbours, but their social isolation was seen as characteristic:[17]

> [Problem families] are a completely new phenomenon, so far as social awareness is concerned. They were not apparent in the general morass of slum life where some degree of child neglect or failure in social upbringing was often caused by large families, combined with slum housing and life below the

8

poverty line. Now, however, the family which fails to raise its standards as these improve all round stands out as an object of social concern.

The term 'problem family' was used so frequently in publications and such a variety of characteristics were ascribed to it that the notion defies succinct definition.[18] However, the general impression was of disorganized family life and irrational, compulsive behaviour by the parents. The theme of recurrent financial crises, such as rent arrears, threatening the family's existence, was often mentioned and the proposal was sometimes made that social workers should have funds to help in these situations. 'Because of low incomes and financial mismanagement the families are usually in need of financial assistance', and 'this must be given immediately if a crisis such as eviction from the home is to be prevented.'[19] It was not sympathy with the families alone which prompted interest in them at this period, but also the exasperation which their difficulties seemed to cause for administration of services such as housing and education.[20]

Ideas on problem families and on methods of working with them had been shaped by the work of the Pacifist Service Units, which had first worked with bombed-out families considered unfit for rehousing. Their caseworkers worked in the home and became involved in the details of family life. Through sharing day to day tasks and giving advice and support in emergencies, the caseworker helped the family to improve its standards. Integral to its work was the building of a relationship and the provision of as much insight as was acceptable to the family, thus enhancing the family's self respect and helping it to cope more rationally.

The idea that many of the clients of the social services were likely to have multiplicities of problems which brought them into touch with several agencies became a major theme in social policy discussion. During the 1950s, a number of influential reports stressed this and called for increased co-ordination of the personal social services. The caseworkers of the Family Service Units (which had developed out of the PSUs), helping families through all of their difficulties demonstrated an alternative model to separated problem-based services and initiated a special role for the social worker in ameliorating problems.[21] As the Association of Children's Officers put the case:[22]

Some families cannot be fitted for a normal life in the community by grants of material aid, or by the work of services that are concerned only with one aspect of their problems. They must in a sense be 'converted' to a new way of life. The only means yet discovered for doing this is the personal influence of someone prepared to help them in every way that is needed.

Although not exclusively related to the work of the children's departments, the theory of the problem family was particularly appropriate to their work. Their functions concerned children who needed either compulsory or voluntary care outside their own homes and this could only be because of breakdown in their families' abilities to care and their isolation from the supports of relatives and neighbours who rally to the help of most families in such contingencies as mothers' confinements. One supposed feature of the problem family was that it perpetuated itself, passing on its pathology to its children. Whatever doubts there might be about public responsibility to extricate adults from their difficulties, there was wide agreement on the value of helping families with problems for the sake of their children.

The Children's Act of 1948 required children's departments to try to restore children in care to their own families. In the 1950s, the growing influence of John Bowlby stressed the importance of family life, even at its most disorganized, for healthy development, and the pathogenic effects of family breakdown in producing social problems, especially delinquency. Children's departments had the highest proportions of staff in local authority personal social services with social work qualifications and many of them aspired to a constructive role in family casework centred on the desirability of retaining the child at home in a healthy environment. A telling argument in favour of this approach, which gained the support of their employing authorities, was that it was cheaper for local authorities than were the consequences of family breaking down.[23] If in order to prevent receptions into care modest outlays could be made to provide essential materials, such as bedding, it would be money providently spent.

Ever since 1948, it had been recognized that, however well regulated the services for children in care might be, social policy which did nothing to prevent the need for care remained deficient.[24] In 1952, a Children and Young Persons (Amendment) Act placed a duty on local authorities to cause enquiries to be made when there was a suggestion that children might need care and protection. Clearly prevention meant ensuring that a child's home was at least minimally adequate in material terms. This might be achieved by influencing the parents to use money coming into the home wisely. Social workers found, however, that work with a family on these lines could be frustrated if debts, particularly rent arrears, had accumulated to the point where the family broke up because of eviction.

Children's departments varied in the extent to which they undertook preventive work. Oxfordshire, from 1952, had someone working on FSU lines with 'hard core problem families'. He gave practical help in home care and, as an alternative to the credit purchase arrangements which the families otherwise used, he sold them bedding and clothing, collecting contributions each week, but not handing over the articles until they were paid for. The worker not only helped the families to provide better care, but demonstrated the advantages of paying for items before they were worn out.[25] (It is not recorded whether the department realized that the families may have been less efficient consumers because they normally had little alternative to expensive credit sale arrangements.) In the same county, when the proportion in care because of homelessness reached 20 per cent, the Children's Committee requested the county to pay rent arrears in some cases, but they were turned down.[26] In Devon, on the other hand, the Children's Department refused applications for care, unless there were other problems affecting the children besides homelessness. There the Welfare Department, which provided temporary accommodation for the homeless, developed its own family casework service. In the Children's Officer's view, before an application for care was received by him, preventive work was the responsibility of health visitors for the 'under fives' and education welfare officers for school children.[27]

By the mid 1950s, however, most children's departments had gone into preventive work and the extent and imaginativeness of this was seen in many quarters, not least by students on training courses, as the measure of a good department. The more of this work the child care officers did, the more they encountered clients' material problems. Some departments responded by building up stores of equipment, such as prams, toys and bedding, which were donated by the public for child care officers to distribute. By and large, however, they could only solve material problems by applications to other agencies such as the National Assistance Board, for those eligible for that benefit, housing departments and other landlords for those with rent arrears or in need of better accommodation, and the Women's Voluntary Service for clothing and equipment and charities. This was time consuming and frustrating when families the social workers wanted to help did not fit the criteria of eligibility of other agencies, or did not happen to gain sympathy from an official who had discretion whether to be helpful or not.

These problems meant that by the late 1950s social workers began pressing for the power to give financial aid themselves. In 1959 one of the major professional journals, *Case Conference*, reported a large volume of correspondence on financial and material aid and ran a series on the topic. The kind of approach taken in much of the correspondence can be illustrated by referring to one particular article. In this article the author, a child care officer, stated:[28]

> It is not practical for any agency to work with problem families unless it is able to provide some material help. These families have exhausted local sources of assistance, and the giving of material help, if undertaken as part of the casework process can yield results far beyond the goods or money given.

The Ingleby Committee

The catalyst for change proved to be the Ingleby Committee. The main part of this Committee's work concerned the constitution and procedure of the juvenile courts and the prevention of cruelty and danger to juveniles. But the second part of their terms of reference, which may have been a late addition,[29] was to consider 'whether local authorities responsible for child care should . . . be given new powers and duties to prevent or forestall the suffering of children through neglect in their own homes'. The Committee, which included no one with any experience in social work, gave its greatest attention to the first part of its remit and was cautious and tentative when dealing with the second. It was clearly unwilling to make any recommendation which might offend any group within the local authorities.

The Committee's report, however, did demonstrate a new approach to the community's responsibility to children and the extent to which local authorities, and therefore social workers, ought to intervene to enhance standards:[30]

> It is not enough to protect children from neglect even if the term neglect be held to include their exposure to any physical, mental or moral danger or deprivation. If children are to be prevented from becoming delinquent, and if those in trouble are to get the help they need, something more positive is required. Everything within reason must be done to ensure not only that children are not neglected but that they get the best upbringing possible. The primary responsibility for bringing up children is parental and it is essentially a positive responsibility. It is the parents' duty to help them to become effective and law abiding citizens by example and training and providing a stable and secure family background in which they can develop satisfactorily. Anything which falls short of this can be said to constitute neglect in the widest sense, although obviously the degree of such neglect which can justify interference by a court must be more rigidly defined and restricted . . . . It is the duty of the community to provide

through its social and welfare services the advice and support which such parents and children need; to build up their sense of responsibility and to enable them to fulfil their proper role. In considering the second part of our terms of reference (namely, whether local authorities responsible for child care should be given new powers and duties to prevent children suffering through neglect in their own homes) we have had this positive aspect of the problem constantly in mind.

The Children and Young Persons Act 1952 had defined the need for care and protection as ill-treatment or neglect likely to cause unnecessary suffering or injury to health and it required local authorities to investigate any report that a child might need care.[31] Ingleby gave child care workers public support for a far wider definition of their role. When, in 1963, local authorities were given a duty to make available such advice, guidance and assistance as might promote the welfare of children and expenditure was allowed for the benefit of children in their own homes, it was clear that in the official view they were expected to be involved with a far wider clientele than previously.

In a possible reference to a contemporary debate caused by Barbara Wootton's castigation of psychoanalytically inspired social work, Ingleby noted that there had been[32]

a certain reaction recently against the indiscriminate application of intensive case-work for family or personal difficulties. From the point of view of the family, or of economy, attention should first be given to the simple forms of social aid.

They accepted the view presented to them in evidence by social work organizations that[33]

for the effective prevention of suffering of children through neglect in their own homes, a skilled intensive case-work service was required (provided either directly by local authorities or through a voluntary agency), and that local authorities should have power to give material assistance where necessary.

The Committee's uneasiness in dealing with local government affairs was apparent in their discussion of the appropriate department in which to place powers regarding children in their own homes. While children's departments were prime contenders, not least because of the preventive work many were already doing, health departments had a claim to be the chief preventive agency and offered health visitors as the appropriate professionals. In the end, the Committee recommended that powers should be vested in local authorities generally without specifying through which committees they should act.

As might be expected, supporters of children's departments argued strongly for the powers to be placed in their hands and when the bill reached Parliament the new duties were given to children's committees. Hence the new power to give financial aid was given to a department in which the social work tradition was paramount. Had it been left to each local authority to decide to whom to delegate these powers, in some areas health visitors, with their especial concern with physical hygiene, would have had them, and in other areas welfare departments which sometimes worked with 'problem families', but had low proportions of trained staffs, would have been given the duties, while in other places all applications for financial aid would have been scrutinized by Clerk's departments, involving a powerful non social work influence. The pattern would have been reconsidered in the later 1960s when the integration of local authority social services was discussed, but by then non social work traditions might have had a continuing influence.

Conclusion

The Ingleby Committee mirrored the change in attitude that had taken place towards financial aid and social work. The firm separation adopted after the Second World War had been attacked by most of the major social work organizations and their spokesmen. The Ingleby Committee essentially had accepted professional opinion and proposed that the barrier between financial aid and social work be lowered, if not broken down.

The Ingleby Committee could only make recommendations; it had no power to make changes itself. Such power was only possessed by Parliament. Nevertheless, the report had a major impact and on the question of financial aid, at least, Parliament followed its lead.

The changes that were taking place over financial aid, of course, were but a small part of the changes affecting the whole range of social services in Britain. The changes in the income maintenance system were particularly important. The assistance based services took over a far wider role than originally had been envisaged. A number of writers have argued that this has had considerable significance for the way financial aid through social work has been used.

Chapter two

Britain: developments since Ingleby

By the early 1960s, then, the climate of opinion in Britain had changed. The complete separation of social work and financial aid was no longer seen to be desirable. The Ingleby Committee had mirrored this view and provided the catalyst for change; the Children and Young Persons Act of 1963 provided the means. The Act ranged widely; the provisions relating to financial aid were made in the first section. Section 1 of the Act stated:[1]

> It shall be the duty of every local authority to make available such advice, guidance and assistance as may promote the welfare of children by diminishing the need to receive children into or keep them in care under the Children Act 1948, the principal Act or the principal Scottish Act or to bring children before a juvenile court; and any provisions made by a local authority under this subsection may, if the local authority think fit, include provision for giving assistance in kind or, in exceptional circumstances cash.

There were three elements to this section: that action should be taken to prevent children (under 18) being taken into care or brought before the courts; that this action could include the provision of financial or material aid; but that financial aid should only be given in exceptional circumstances.

Further guidance about the way these new powers might be used was available from two sources. In Parliament, during the debate on the Bill the Minister had outlined the way the new powers including material aid could be used to keep children out of care:[2]

> [Help] could be intensive social case work. It could be a matter of providing practical help to a mother who cannot cope with the burden of a large family. It could be paying off arrears of rent so that the children do not have to come into care because

15

of eviction. It could be a matter of lending household equipment to a family who does not have adequate equipment or it could be a matter of advising responsible parents who feel that a teenage daughter is getting beyond their control.

Subsequent to the passing of the 1963 Act the Home Office issued a circular to local authorities[3] outlining how the new powers should be used in more detail. A number of limitations were stressed: the new powers were not intended to permit local authorities to undertake work which had been the province of the National Assistance Board, they were not intended to permit local authorities to force assistance or casework on unwilling clients and cash was only to be given directly to clients in 'exceptional circumstances' (this last point was a reiteration of the provision of the Act). The circular also stressed the desirability of liaison between the local authority department and a variety of other agencies, including the church, housing authorities and voluntary organizations. It quoted an example of possible liaison with the last mentioned type of body. The local authority might make arrangements for a voluntary organization to give advice, guidance and assistance on their behalf and repay them for any expenditure necessarily incurred; 'for example a payment might be made to a voluntary organisation to meet the cost of transporting and storing furniture given by the general public to help families in difficulty'.[4] However, the circular stopped short of issuing specific instructions on specific issues: it did not list the ways that the new powers might be used or the procedures that might be followed. This was to be left to individual local authorities to determine. And it stressed that the new Act gave clients no new 'rights'. Thus, in an appendix to the circular it was stated: 'Benefits in kind or cash are included as the local authority think fit and therefore cannot be claimed as of right'.[5]

Early experience with financial aid

Table 1 shows the amounts given in financial aid under the terms of the 1963 Act in England between 1965 and 1970. From this table it can be seen that initially very little aid was given at all. In 1965-6 only about £60,000 was given and by 1968-9 the total was still less than a quarter of a million pounds. There seem to have been two reasons for this. First, some local authorities only budgeted for very small amounts of expenditure. One study reported that an authority they looked at only budgeted for £50 in the first year. Second, although in some ways Section 1 had been introduced as the result of pressure from social workers many of them had no clear idea about how they should use their new powers.

16

Table 1   Financial aid given in England under Section 1 of the Children and Young Persons Act 1963, 1965-70

Year	Amount (£)
1965-6	66,600
1966-7	135,100
1967-8	188,800
1968-9	244,900
1969-70	377,000

Source: Home Office

By 1966 the Home Office clearly believed that their earlier exhortation that financial aid should only be given in exceptional circumstances was being taken too literally: in a new circular issued in that year they urged local authorities 'to be bold in their application of the Act'.[6] Whether this new instruction had any direct effect is difficult to tell; nevertheless there is no doubt that expenditure on financial aid increased dramatically in subsequent years. By the end of the 1960s it was about five times the 1965-6 level. Even after allowing for inflation the increases recorded were dramatic.

Of course, these figures are aggregate and conceal tremendous variations: the variations between different local authorities will be examined later but it might be worth while commenting on the differences between England and Scotland in the 1960s at this juncture. Expenditure on financial aid under the 1963 Act in Scotland was £12,000 in 1965-6 and £63,000 in 1969. If one calculates expenditure per head of the population then this means that it was about twice as high in Scotland as in England in 1965-6 and about three times as high in 1969.

However, the crude total amount of aid given was by no means the only difference between England and Scotland. Just as important were the differences in the way it was given.

Comprehensive figures were collected by the Scottish Education Department in 1969 on the reasons for which Scottish social workers gave financial aid. These figures are reproduced in Table 2. From this table it can be seen that 41 per cent of aid was given to cover arrears of rent or rates and 35 per cent was given to cover gas, water or electricity accounts. Unfortunately such comprehensive figures are not available for England and Wales. However, some guidance about the position can be obtained from Heywood and Allen's study.[7] This was undertaken in the late 1960s in four northern authorities. It revealed that in three of the authorities the major reason for aid was to enable clients to purchase food. In the fourth

17

Britain: developments since Ingleby

Table 2   Reasons for granting financial aid under Section 1 of
the Children and Young Persons Act 1963, in Scotland, 1969

Reason for aid	Number of families	Total expenditure £	Repayment of those assisted £
Payment of fares	153	492	41
Arrears of rent and/or rates	1,234	26,037	9,767
Payment of gas, water or electricity accounts	1,304	21,933	8,694
Direct cash payments:			
(i) to meet hire purchase commitments	24	264	137
(ii) other payments	453	4,253	1,349
Other assistance	496	7,285	690
Total	3,664	60,264	20,678

Source: Scottish Education Department, *Social Work in Scotland 1969*,
HMSO, Edinburgh, 1970, Cmnd 4475

authority the major reason for aid was to enable clients to pay rent arrears; the purchase of food was the second most frequent reason. Relatively little money was given to deal with fuel debts. Heywood and Allen never claimed that their authorities were typical: nevertheless, the other evidence that exists suggests that although there were variations between authorities (in central London many boroughs had to deal with particular housing problems with the result that they spent substantial sums on bed and breakfast accommodation which at that time seemed to be peculiar to their areas) the bulk of aid was given for food and household necessities.

The differences noted between the English and Scottish use of financial aid are not easy to explain. The high proportion of aid given to pay rent arrears in Scotland is particularly puzzling given the traditionally low level of Scottish rents (in 1968, for example, council house rents in Glasgow averaged little over sixteen shillings a week). The higher payments for fuel and water debts are not quite so perplexing but are still not easy to explain because although total fuel bills might be higher in Scotland than in England, in certain areas at least many houses in the late 1960s had more than one source of fuel and social workers have been reluctant to give aid in the past if only one of a number of sources of fuel available has been threatened because of arrears.

An explanation for the apparent variations in practice between

18

England and Scotland however might be found by looking at a number of factors. First, a number of people have claimed that in the past the Supplementary Benefits Commission has been less willing to give exceptional needs grants for fuel and rent arrears in Scotland than in England. Second, other public bodies, especially housing and fuel authorities may have put greater pressure on, and had more success in persuading, social workers in Scotland to use their powers to pay fuel and rent debts. There is little doubt that once such bodies have made inroads on this matter it is easy for the position to be exploited and difficult for social workers to reverse the trend. Third, Scottish social workers, as Carmichael argues,[8] may have had less firm ideas about how financial aid should be used and therefore it may have been easier for housing and fuel authorities to persuade them to look towards matters like fuel and rent.

Before we leave this issue a note of caution ought to be sounded: there may be some discrepancy between the reason for which financial aid was 'officially' given and the reason for which it was really given. An example might help to illuminate this point. A case was related to us of a client who approached a social work department for help to pay a court fine. The woman concerned was a young mother living alone with four children and, had she been unable to pay the fine and been committed to prison, the local authority would have had to take her children into care (at considerable expense). The social worker concerned decided that it was justifiable in the circumstances to use local authority finance to pay the fine but realized that if she recorded that she had used Section 1 money to pay a fine, such a course of action would be unacceptable. Instead the social worker instructed the client not to pay her electricity bill and to use the money saved to pay her fine. Help was thus recorded as having been given to pay a fuel debt when the court fine was the precipitating problem.

More recent developments

There have been a number of other developments since 1963 in England and Wales which have affected the ability of social workers to give financial and material aid to their clients. Local authority social work departments have increased the scope of their aid to clients both in terms of the amount of aid given and the type of client aided. Clients are now aided, for example, through the Health Services and Public Health Act 1968 and through the Chronically Sick and Disabled Persons Act 1970. It is clear, however, that even though many of these developments are an extension of previous practice, they are still limited. For example, although the Health Services and Public Health Act of 1968 says that a[9]

19

Britain: developments since Ingleby

> local authority may with the approval of the Minister of Health, and to such an extent as he may direct, shall make arrangements for promoting the welfare of old people

it also says that[10]

> No arrangement under this section shall provide — (a) for the payment of money to old people except in so far as the arrangements may provide for the remuneration of old people engaged in suitable work in accordance with arrangements.

It is also clear that most of the aid given is not direct financial but material aid.

The increase in the use of Section 1 of the 1963 Act noted for the late 1960s has continued in the 1970s and is still the most important aspect of financial aid. Table 3 shows expenditure under Section 1 of the 1963 Act in England between 1970 and 1975. From this table it can be seen that in 1971-2 expenditure was about ten times the level in 1965-6 and almost twice the level in 1969-70; between 1972-3 and 1973-4 expenditure increased by about 70 per cent and between 1973-4 and 1974-5 it increased by about 40 per cent. All these increases are far more than could be accounted for by inflation.

Part of the explanation for these increases can be seen by looking at the reasons for which the money has been given. The evidence available suggests that the pattern noted for the 1960s changed in the 1970s: in some ways the English position moved much closer to that in Scotland. This can be seen from a number of different sources.

The Department of Health and Social Security attempted to collect comprehensive statistics on the reasons for the use of financial aid through social work in England in 1974-5 and 1975-6.

Table 3 Financial aid given in England under Section 1 of the Children and Young Persons Act 1963, 1970-75

Year	Amount £
1970-1	534,000
1971-2	652,000
1972-3*	1,431,000
1973-4*	2,429,000
1974-5*	3,450,000

*These figures include payments made under other headings and are therefore not directly comparable with those for the earlier periods
Source: Home Office, Department of Health and Social Security, Health and Personal Social Service Statistics for England

20

Unfortunately their efforts were largely frustrated because many authorities lumped the bulk of their payments under the 'other' heading. Consequently the Department has now abandoned the collection of such statistics. However, other studies, if partial, are rather more illuminating. Hawker and Emmett, in their research for the British Association of Social Workers Poverty Group,[11] looked in detail at expenditure under Section 1 of the 1963 Act in twelve London boroughs. Their results are summarized in Table 4. From this table it can be seen that in three of the boroughs over 70 per cent of all aid was given for bed and breakfast. There is little doubt that these boroughs were not unique in making large payments for bed and breakfast accommodation. In some authorities payment has been made under powers other than those granted by Section 1 of the 1963 Act. However, the problems with which bed and breakfast payments are meant to deal are concentrated in certain areas, largely the older city districts. Possibly the most interesting statistics are those relating to fuel debts: in half of the boroughs payments to cover fuel debts accounted for more than 40 per cent of the total aid.

Other studies have confirmed the growing emphasis in Section 1 payments on help with fuel debts. For example, Ross in a study of financial aid in the York area[12] found that over half the expenditure was to meet fuel debts. While it is important to remember that these figures are far from comprehensive and the recorded may not always be the real reason for the aid, it does appear as if there has been an increase in the problems caused by fuel debts and there is little doubt that these problems are linked to the rise in the cost of fuel in the early 1970s.

Recent developments in Scotland

The growth and development of the use of financial aid through social work in England and Wales has to all intents and purposes been within the terms of Section 1 of the 1963 Act. Recent developments in Scotland have been under the provisions of new legislation, the Social Work (Scotland) Act of 1968, which has considerably increased the scope of the original statute.

The 1968 Social Work (Scotland) Act was the culmination of a lengthy period of debate about social work in Scotland. The debate had its origins in the work of the McBoyle Committee on the Prevention of Neglect of Children which reported[13] only four months after the 1963 Children and Young Persons Act reached the statute book. Although the report had little direct influence on legislation it was the start of a period of innovation in Scottish social work. Prior to 1960 personal social services in Scotland in general lagged behind those in England in terms of services and the qualifications of staff.

Table 4 Reasons for expenditure (under Section 1 of the 1963 Act) on Supplementary Benefits claimants in twelve London boroughs

		Fuel %	Food %	Clothing %	Furniture %	Rent arrears %	Bed and breakfast %	Fuel debts %
Inner London boroughs	(1)*	—	18·43	10·13	3·25	7·18	3·21	41·77
	(2)	—	—	—	6·85	2·32	—	31·26
	(3)†	—	20·66	10·21	3·75	8·01	—	38·32
	(4)	—	1·82	0·26	2·28	2·44	85·04	4·73
Outer London boroughs	(5)	2·74	6·29	0·31	1·48	—	71·88	7·86
	(6)	2·09	14·68	2·06	7·55	—	0·33	44·99
	(7)	2·91	3·04	1·09	0·91	—	73·83	15·34
	(8)	—	3·59	—	5·98	9·97	2·21	68·24
	(9)	—	8·60	1·75	—	6·14	—	35·61
	(10)	—	4·47	4·25	—	19·16	—	51·66
	(11)	—	21·71	1·66	7·57	4·16	—	42·03
	(12)	4·18	2·87	2·91	7·13	14·07	—	59·52

*Figures cover one three month period only
†Figures relate to one area team
Source: M. Hawker and T. Emmett, Survey in the London Boroughs of Section 1, Children and Young Persons Act 1963 Payments, British Association of Social Workers Poverty Group, London, 1974

The debate was continued by the Kilbrandon Committee and a White Paper on the reorganization of social work.[14] This latter document provided the basis for the 1968 Act.

The Social Work (Scotland) Act of 1968 was a major piece of legislation influencing the organization of social work departments and juvenile justice in Scotland. Two sections of the Act, 12 and 24, made special reference to the question of financial aid. Section 12 of the Social Work (Scotland) Act said:[15]

It shall be the duty of every local authority to promote social welfare by making available advice, guidance and assistance on such a scale as may be appropriate for their area.

It was made clear that the 'promotion of welfare' could be achieved through the provision of financial aid, though as one of the architects of the Act has since commented, 'money was never intended to be an important aspect of Section 12.[16] This was made clear in the Act by the stipulation that financial aid was only to be given 'in exceptional circumstances constituting an emergency' and was only to be given if it[17]

would avoid the local authority being caused greater expense in the giving of assistance in another form or where probable aggravation of the person's need would cause expense to the local authority on another occasion.

Nevertheless, Section 12 was an important extension of the 1963 Act in that it permitted local authorities to give aid to promote the welfare of sections of the community other than children. It is also clear that financial aid to individuals has become a major, if not the major, use of expenditure under Section 12.

Section 24 gave social work departments the power to take action in a much more specialized area. Under the terms of this section departments were given the power to offer grants to people who had been in the care of the authority and continued their education after the age of eighteen.

Table 5 gives details of the amount of aid given by social work departments in Scotland under the terms of Sections 12 and 24 of the 1968 Act between 1970 and 1974. From this table it can be seen that in 1970 £212,000 was given or loaned to clients; this might be compared to the total of £60,264 in the last year before the operation of the 1968 Act. The threefold increase between the immediate pre and the immediate post period of operation of the 1968 Act is far greater than can be explained by reference to inflation or developments of the kind taking place in England (although a direct comparison with the English situation is not possible because of the

Table 5 Financial aid through social work under the provisions of the Social Work (Scotland) Act 1968, 1970-4

Year	Section 12 aid		Section 24 aid		Total	
	Number assisted	Total payment £	Number assisted	Total payment £	Number assisted	Total payment £
1970	14,448	212,000	266	32,400	14,714	244,400
1971	17,592	196,500	165	18,800	17,757	215,300
1972	19,716	233,700	164	17,000	19,880	250,700
1973	20,316	236,300	175	18,000	20,491	254,300
1974	26,106	384,540	210	24,908	26,316	409,448

Source: Scottish Education Department, Social Work Services Group, Scottish Social Work Statistics

Table 6 Reasons for which financial aid was given under the Social Work (Scotland) Act 1968, 1970-4

Year	Gas arrears		Electricity arrears and deposits		Rent arrears		Other payments		Total	
	Numbers assisted	Total payment £	Numbers assisted	Total payment £	Numbers assisted	Total payment £	Numbers assisted	Total payment £	Numbers assisted	Total payment £
1970	–	–	–	–	–	–	–	–	14,448	212,000
1971	715	10,271	5,790	74,386	–	–	11,087	111,843	17,592	196,500
1972	588	36,402	10,798	64,209	–	–	8,330	133,089	19,716	233,700
1973	1,296	18,142	4,394	72,024	5,313	78,953	9,313	67,181	20,316	236,300
1974	1,536	14,044	5,258	98,983	4,293	177,904	15,019	93,609	26,106	384,540

Source: Scottish Education Department, Social Work Services Group

different accounting periods, the percentage increase in the amount of financial aid given through social work in Scotland was more than double that in England). The assumption must be that the increase in the expenditure on financial aid in 1970 was partly, if not largely, the result of the widening of the powers under the 1968 Act. This view is reinforced when one notes that in the following year the amount spent on financial aid decreased slightly, and in the two years after increased, but by a relatively small percentage (if inflation and total social work budgets are taken into account then expenditure decreased in 1972 and 1973 as well). It was only in 1974 that the trend towards swiftly rising expenditure on financial aid was regained.

Table 6 shows the reasons for which financial aid was given through social work in Scotland during the early 1970s. From this table it can be seen that, in general terms, the pre 1970s pattern seems to have been maintained. However, two more specific points might be noted. First, by 1973 fuel not rent arrears had become the major cause of financial aid. This could be linked to developments in England, where higher fuel costs had caused major problems and to the acquisition since 1968 of a new group of clients (the elderly) who were especially susceptible to fuel problems. Second, in 1974 the position was dramatically reversed. Payments to meet fuel debts increased by about £22,000 but payments to meet rent arrears increased far faster, almost by £100,000. Thus by 1974 almost 50 per cent of all expenditure under Section 12 was designed to cover rent arrears and the major increase in total expenditure on financial aid can largely be accounted for by rent debt payments. It is worth while noting that this period saw the major impact of the rent rises in many urban areas in Scotland as a result of the Housing Finance Act.

Conclusion

The Children and Young Persons Act of 1963 gave social workers the power to offer financial aid directly to clients. After a slow start, these new powers were used widely and today social workers are handling about four million pounds. In some ways, though, the sums involved are the least important part of the picture. Far more crucial is the reason for which money has been given. In England and Wales initially a high proportion was given for food, clothing and household necessities but of late fuel and rent debts have increased in importance; in Scotland they have always been the most important items. This has raised a major area of debate. Many social workers claim that currently financial aid is not being used in the way anticipated (as part of a general social work strategy) but as a way of helping clients to deal with problems created by other public agencies. Such claims have been brought into focus of late by the considerable increase in fuel and rent charges. Social workers have also questioned the extent to which the problems clients present should be the responsibility of the Supplementary Benefits Commission. Many have argued that the Commission and its staff often direct clients to social service and social work departments because they want to reduce their workload, rather than because the clients really need social work assistance.

Chapter three

Relationships between social work and other public agencies

Local authority personal social service departments have never been able to work and could never work in isolation. Their task has often brought them into contact with other agencies. Sometimes this contact has taken the form of co-operative ventures: this has happened frequently with bodies like voluntary associations and the churches. On occasions staff employed in social service and social work departments have had cause to contact other agencies on behalf of their clients: in effect, they have become intermediaries or sometimes advocates for their clients. There has also been contact between personal social service departments and other agencies in order to ensure that their work is complementary rather than competing: this has sometimes led to concern about the boundaries between agencies.

Contact of the kind mentioned above is not new and certainly existed before the introduction of the 1963 Children and Young Persons Act. However, Section 1 of the Act called for greater co-operation between children's departments and other agencies: the reference in the Home Office circular (issued following the introduction of the Act) to the need for greater co-operation between children's departments and voluntary organizations has already been noted. Section 1 of the Act also highlighted and in some instances exacerbated the problems of the boundaries between local authority personal social service departments and other agencies. The friction that has developed, in some places largely as a result of the power to give financial aid, between personal social service departments and three other public agencies (the Supplementary Benefits Commission, housing departments and the fuel authorities) is particularly important and worthy of detailed consideration.

Relationships between social work and other public agencies

Supplementary Benefits Commission

Role of the Commission

The British social security system has its origins in the Beveridge Report published in November 1942.[1] The aim of the report was to establish a social security system which would ensure that all members of the community would be 'free from want'. The Beveridge scheme for social security was based on three main elements. First, a system of social insurance which would provide benefits on a contractual basis. Second, a system of child allowances which would offer benefit to all without any contributory or means test conditions. Third, a system of social assistance which would be a 'safety net' for all who fell through the mesh of social insurance. Social assistance was to be provided in relation to need and on the basis of a test of means.

Although in general terms the Beveridge Report laid the foundations for the modern British 'welfare state' the plan was by no means followed in every detail and subsequently major changes have taken place. As far as social assistance is concerned this task was initially assigned to the National Assistance Board, but since 1966 it has been undertaken by the Supplementary Benefits Commission, a body with much closer links to the main government 'social service department', the Department of Health and Social Security. Beveridge believed that social assistance would have to deal with a small and diminishing minority: the largest group dealt with would be elderly people who had not built up sufficient contributions to obtain an adequate insurance based state pension. In fact, the Supplementary Benefits Commission has had to deal with in excess of four million people and their role in many instances has not been to provide a safety net for those who have slipped through the insurance mesh but to 'top up' inadequate insurance benefits. Over the years changes have taken place in the make up of the clientele. The proportion of elderly has declined and today about a third are one parent families and over 20 per cent are unemployed.

The bulk of the work of the SBC is tied up with the provision of fixed rate supplementary pensions and allowances payable on a weekly basis to persons who are not in full time work and whose resources fall short of their requirements. Formally, the levels of such benefits are fixed by Parliament. No doubt the chairman of the Supplementary Benefits Commission has been able to make suggestions and recommendations; nevertheless, the Commission has had little formal power. Since 1975 scale rates have been subject to annual review in order to take account of changing economic conditions, in particular the level of inflation.

28

As far as the scale allowances are concerned, then, subject to the discussion above, the SBC assesses need according to predetermined criteria and its principal task is the fairly mechanical administration of the system. Of course, no body of rules can cover every eventuality and there is always room for discretion on the part of officials when assessing 'means' and 'needs'[2] but it is fair to argue that discretion is at a minimum in this area. Initially (when the National Assistance Board was set up) it was believed that discretion, in any part of the system, was undesirable; this was a reflection of the 'crude universalism' of the period. However, the need to exercise discretion was reluctantly accepted and by the end of its life the National Assistance Board was making discretionary payments to large proportions of its clients. When the Ministry of Social Security was set up attempts were made to reduce the need to provide regular discretionary payments: central to this move was the introduction of standard long term additions to scale rates. The Supplementary Benefits Commission was still to have the power to increase the scale rates in exceptional circumstances (through the system of exceptional circumstances payments), but it was assumed that because of the introduction of the standard long term additions such payments would be made far less frequently than in the past. At first this expectation was fulfilled: in 1967 only 594,000 exceptional circumstances payments were made compared to 1,157,000 in 1965. However, the position changed in subsequent years, so that by 1975 over one million exceptional circumstances payments were made.[3] The major reason for the increase in such payments seems to have been the rise in applications for assistance with heating bills. The Social Security Act of 1966 as well as giving the Supplementary Benefits Commission the power to make regular additions to scale rates also gave them the power to make discretionary lump sum payments; these were provided for in the system of exceptional needs and emergency needs payments, dealt with in Sections 7 and 13 of the Act.

Section 7 of the 1966 Act states:

where it appears to the Commission reasonable in all the circumstances they may determine that benefit shall be paid to a person by way of a single payment to meet an exceptional need.

The powers granted to the SBC under Section 7 are wide and have been used increasingly of late. Table 7 shows the number of payments made and the amount of help given under this heading: it can be seen that whereas in 1968 fewer than 500,000 payments were made and the total expenditure was about £2¾ million, by 1976 more than double the number of payments were made and expen-

Table 7 Exceptional needs payments, 1968-75

	Number of payments	Average payment £	Total payment £000s
1968	470,000	5·80	2,726
1969	500,000	6·19	3,095
1970	560,000	6·86	3,842
1971	576,000	8·18	4,711
1972	743,000	9·54	7,088
1973	808,000	11·51	9,300
1974	830,000	13·85	11,496
1975	945,000	18·18	17,180
1976	1,114,000	21·56	24,023

Source: Department of Health and Social Security, Social Security Statistics

diture was over £24 million. A survey of exceptional needs payments made in 1968[4] gave some idea of the kinds of reason for which such payments were made: 56·9 per cent of all payments and 50·4 per cent of all expenditure was given for clothing and footwear, 16·7 per cent of all payments and 22·9 per cent of all expenditure was given for bedding, furniture and household goods and 4·5 per cent of all payments and 5·9 per cent of expenditure was given for gas, coal or electricity bills. Although the level of expenditure had increased dramatically since 1968 the pattern of expenditure had not altered markedly. In 1975 58·3 per cent of all payments were for clothing and footwear, 21·6 per cent were for bedding, furniture and household goods and 9 per cent were for fuel.

Section 13 of the 1966 Act states:

> Nothing . . . shall prevent the payment of benefit in an urgent case, and in determining whether any benefit is payable and the amount or nature of the benefit, the Commission shall not be bound by anything in Schedule 2 to this Act [it sets out provisions for determining the right to and level of benefit] or in any regulations made under this Act which appears to them inappropriate in the circumstances of the case.

The powers granted to the Commission by this section, as with Section 7, thus are wide; further it is stated in one subsection that the powers to make emergency payments extend to those who would not normally be able to claim benefit under the Supplementary Benefits Scheme (in particular, those in full time work). However, emergency payments are given more frequently to people already in receipt of supplementary benefits who had encountered problems because of administrative difficulties involving the Commission itself: new claimants may have to wait for their claims to be processed and benefit giros may have been lost or held up.

The Supplementary Benefits Scheme as a whole is built on the notion of 'rights', the 'rights' of clients to benefits. This 'right' is most clearly visible with the scale benefits but extends in theory to the discretionary benefits as well (the difficulty in marrying the notion of rights with that of discretion is not hard to appreciate). In an attempt to control administrative discretion and ensure that it is not misused by its officials the Supplementary Benefits Commission introduced a code of rules (known as the 'A' code) to guide its employees. This code has never been made generally available to the public but a handbook outlining the broad principles applied has been published instead. Senior members of the Board also, at various times, have indicated how policy is applied and the constraints they feel that they are under. Thus, the Chairman of the Supplementary Benefits Commission has stated:[5]

> It would clearly be wrong for the Commission to exercise their
> discretionary powers to make lump sum payments so
> indiscriminately as to improve artificially the living standards
> which Parliament had sought to provide when fixing the scale
> rates.

It has also been argued that the Commission cannot provide help, on the basis of a loan, where continuing help is needed or where the problem is mismanagement rather than inadequate resources. At other times it has been made clear that the Commission cannot normally make double payments: that is, payments which relate to an item already covered in the scale rates (such as fuel or rent).[6]

The boundary with social work

Since the introduction of the 1963 Children and Young Persons Act it has been clear that there has existed potential for overlap and conflict between the Supplementary Benefits Commission and social service departments. Both are able to make discretionary payments to clients and frequently clients of one agency are also clients of the other. In an attempt to avert this conflict, the Home Office circular issued following the introduction of the Act amplified the bare statement in Section 1. Thus it said:[7]

> It is not intended that the power to give material assistance
> under Section 1 of the Act should be used to provide an
> alternative to National Assistance or a child care supplement to

Relationships between social work and other public agencies

> National Assistance payments—continuing payments would in any event have to be taken into account as a resource by the Board in deciding the amount of regular National Assistance grant. It will therefore be necessary for the authority to arrange close liaison with the National Assistance Board to ensure that assistance, whether in kind or in cash, is not given in circumstances where it could more appropriately be given by the Board or where the result would be an unjustifiable duplication of expenditure from public funds.

The memorandum went on to suggest that local authority departments should always contact the National Assistance Board before giving aid unless the head of the household of the recipient was in full time employment.

Of course, the picture was still far from clear. The Home Office memorandum spelt out the dangers in more detail than the Act and counselled in favour of co-operation but failed to lay down detailed guidelines. The same comment might be made about the Social Work (Scotland) Act 1968. Subsection 3 stated that Section 12 powers to grant financial aid should not be used where there were other statutory bodies that could make payments but no specific guidelines or detailed policy were suggested. Yet, clearly, detailed guidelines were needed if conflict was to be avoided. While it is relatively easy to define the major aims and responsibilities of the assistance agency on the one hand, and the social services and social work departments on the other, it is far more difficult to define the boundary of their interests precisely and thus ensure that overlap does not occur. Further, the exhortation in the Acts and memoranda in favour of co-operation and consultation were only of limited value. The two organizations are based on different assumptions and philosophies. The personnel of one organization often find it difficult to understand and sympathize with the motives of the other. In such circumstances, co-operation and consultation are often empty phrases which do little more than paper over the inadequacy and lack of clarity of policy decisions.

The debate about the division of responsibilities for financial aid between the social service and social work departments and the Supplementary Benefits Commission has intensified of late and become increasingly acrimonious. Most of the charges have been made by social workers or sympathetic writers who believe that social workers have been forced to take over much of the work of the SBC to the detriment of the original aims of Section 1 of the 1963 Act. The charges can be narrowed down to three main areas of complaint.

The first area of complaint concerns emergency financial aid. One of the main protagonists in the debate has been Bill Jordan. He has argued[8] that social workers increasingly have been forced to take over the responsibility of the Supplementary Benefits Commission for emergency payments because of the centralization of that organization. He cites as evidence the increasing amount of the business of the SBC being carried out by post (giros are posted to claimants rather than handed out over the counter in most areas), the closure of many local offices, and the reduction in opening hours. He says:[9]

> Ever since 1966, when the Ministry of Social Security came into existence, it has become progressively more difficult for claimants to get money to meet urgent need. First came the giro system, which abolished cash payments over the counter; now we have the rapid closure of local offices, and their substitution by 'call points' dispensing advice but neither money nor giros. To make claim for immediate need, the destitute person is likely to have to undertake a considerable and expensive journey, only to be told that he must await a money order by the next morning's post. In many areas, visiting systems are being reduced to such an extent that it seems reasonable to suppose that the D.H.S.S. intends eventually to phase them out altogether, and to carry on its business by post.

According to Jordan, the centralization of the SBC organization has itself been both the cause of many of the emergencies that have to be dealt with and the reason why the SBC cannot deal with the emergencies themselves. Centralization has meant the payment of benefit by post, which has resulted in a less reliable service, as well as the reduction of facilities available to deal with problems when they arise.

The SBC has made arrangements to try to deal with the problems caused by centralization and the restricted opening hours of their offices. One of the arrangements has been to appoint officers who can be contacted at home out of office hours in an emergency. However, the system has a major drawback: in order to recruit officers the SBC has had to agree that they will not have to make themselves available at all times or be 'on call'; they will merely deal with problems if they are contacted.

In some areas social work departments seem to have accepted that they should offer an emergency service if one is not provided by the SBC. The Social Work Services Group in a circular to Scottish local authorities stated:[10]

> With the creation of area offices of the Social Work
> Departments, it will happen, on occasions that a person in

urgent need will apply to the local Social Work Department office for assistance, and it will often not be practicable for him to be sent to the local Social Security office, because of the distance between the offices, the time of the day or the urgency of the circumstances.

In some English areas arrangements have been made for social work departments to provide an emergency out of hours service and then claim back payments made from the SBC. However, the SBC does not guarantee to make repayments: it will only do so in cases where they believe they should accept responsibility.

A second area of complaint concerns the exercise of discretion. Many social workers believe that the SBC is trying to reduce the number of its discretionary payments and persuade social service and social work departments to take over responsibility in such areas.

There is little doubt that the SBC finds discretion difficult to handle. The organization is structured on firm bureaucratic lines: the rules governing scale rates are a testimony to this. Staff, by and large, are not expected to exercise their own judgment in deciding benefit levels and are not trained to do so. Even the areas of discretion it admits are covered by codes and rules of practice. The Commission employs special officials to deal with certain types of case: the appointment of special welfare officers and social work advisers indicated a desire to take account of the 'welfare' nature of some of its work but the system has not been extended significantly nor does it seem to impinge on the bulk of the organization.

Recently, David Donnison, Chairman of the Supplementary Benefits Commission, has presented plans for the further reduction of the discretion exercised by the Commission.[11] He argues that the use of discretion by the Commission on the present scale has a number of unpalatable results. One is the growth of guidelines to show staff how to use their powers. The rules have become 'increasingly complicated, incomprehensible and unpublishable'. This has led to the erosion of confidence in the scheme—'the confidence of claimants that they have clearly defined rights, the confidence of staff that they are getting extra money to those who really need it most, and the confidence of the public that we are being fair to claimants and non-claimants alike'.[12] Other results include the growth in the number of appeals against Commission decisions, and distraction from consideration of the adequacy of scale rates. Donnison also argues that the use of discretion by the Commission may have harmed one particular group of claimants, the unemployed. He suggests that their need for discretionary payments is often less obvious than that of other groups (like the

34

elderly) and they tend to fare less well when they appeal against discretionary decisions which go against them.

Olive Stevenson has provided an extensive discussion of the role of discretion in an assistance agency.[13] She has noted that the removal of discretion altogether may result in the development of rules and tightly defined categories to such an extent that the agency fails to fulfil its functions properly. While recognizing the dangers of 'too much discretion' and the need, emphasized by Titmuss, for claimants to be aware of their rights in relation to an assistance agency, she still argues that discretion cannot and should not be eliminated altogether. As social work adviser to the Supplementary Benefits Commission she has been in an influential position to forward such ideas.

The debate is taken a stage further by Jordan who argues that Donnison's attack on discretion fails to recognize that the SBC operates two different kinds of discretion. One is the discretion to give an extra heating or dietary allowance which is provided on a regular weekly basis: the other is the discretion to make a single payment to cover an urgent or exceptional circumstance. It may well be possible to regularize or systematize the former: at the moment the allowances are usually paid according to a fixed scale. However, he argues that it will be impossible to abolish the latter kind of discretionary payment without hurting an important section of the SBC's clientele. Thus Jordan says:[14]

> Since supplementary benefits are confined to those with very low incomes and little or no savings, they are of necessity concerned with people who have few resources to meet unexpected circumstances. For people on the poverty line the recurrence of substantial regular commitments is hard enough to manage successfully, and the simultaneous arrival of two large bills, even if they were both anticipated, can be impossible.
> So much the less can any such family plan for every new circumstance, or allow for each possible need, least of all for the special needs of young children, the sick, the disabled and the elderly frail. Providing for such eventualities as these for people who have no margin for error is a main function of the Supplementary Benefits scheme.

Nevertheless, it is clear that there is considerable pressure from other sources to reduce the extent of discretion in the operation of the Supplementary Benefits Scheme. Of course, the Chairman of the SBC argues that any reduction in the discretion exercised by the Commission will not be passed on to social work departments. His argument is that entitlement to benefits as of right should replace a great deal of discretion and that social work departments need not be involved. However, in the past considerable concern has been expressed about the way that SBC officers have referred clients to social work departments. The belief has become widespread that a referral to a social work department has been a means of passing on the responsibility for exercising discretion. Thus, one report on the provision of financial aid through social work has examined the instructions the SBC gives to its officials and argued that it[15]

> stresses in a number of places the value it places on
> co-operation with local Social Service Departments but in
> practice, the 'referrals' and 'consultations' referred to tend to
> take the form of a blunt refusal to help and the suggestion that
> the claimant try the Social Services Department.

A number of commentators have also been concerned about the passive role adopted by SBC officers in the exercise of discretion. In particular, officers appear to wait for clients to claim extra benefits rather than recommend their provision in relevant cases. This is well illustrated by a study of the elderly in Coventry[16] which showed that such clients were not given discretionary payments by the SBC, even though they were entitled to them, simply because they had not made a specific request. Further, most of the clients had inadequate knowledge of their rights in this area and had not been briefed by SBC officers.

There is little doubt, however, that though many social workers and their spokesmen today complain that the SBC is trying to avoid responsibility for discretion, in the past (and this is still true in some quarters today) others have argued that the SBC as an organization is not suited to the exercise of discretion and have claimed this as their own province. The SBC officer has been typified as an unsympathetic and insensitive bureaucrat who should not be permitted to meddle in the 'personal' problems of clients. A number of studies[17] have highlighted the prejudices of social security officials and this has strengthened the belief that they should not be permitted to exercise their own judgment. It is difficult to be certain how widely such views were or are held or what part they have played in the transfer of discretion from the social security to the social work agency, but their existence highlights the dilemmas and contradictions inherent in discussion in this area.

The third area of complaint concerns the adequacy of scale rates. The basis of the complaint is that clients face difficulties with payments for fuel and rent and the like, not, as the SBC frequently claims, because of mismanagement, but because of inadequacy of finance. The problem in essence, it is argued, is one of poverty and the relief of poverty should be the province of the SBC. Poverty can be related to two factors: first and foremost it is related to the economic structure of society, the level of wages and the like, but secondly and more specifically, for clients of the SBC, it is related to the inadequacy of scale benefits. This latter problem has been brought into focus of late by the controversy surrounding fuel debts. The SBC scale rates contain an element to cover fuel, but unlike the element to cover rent, it is not related to the particular circumstances in which the family find themselves. As a result, expenditure on fuel frequently may be far in excess of that expected and allowed for, particularly since the rise in fuel costs and the increasing use of central heating in council houses.[18] The leader of a social work team in one of Scotland's major cities illustrated the problem when he reviewed the situation on a large new council housing estate where all of the houses had either gas warm air or electric night store heating. He concluded:[19]

> The cost of electricity for a family needing hot water ten hours per day and cooking by electricity, in a house with night store heating averages £4.90 per week over the year on the new tariff. The proportion of the S.B. allowance for heating, hot water, lighting and cooking is £1.70. Where is the other £3.20 to come from?

The reply of the SBC is that the adequacy of the scale rates is outside their control: they are fixed by Parliament and as has already been noted the SBC claims that it would be wrong for them to try to use their powers of discretion to frustrate the wishes of Parliament. However, the position is complicated by the argument of writers like Jordan[20] who suggest that the inadequacy of the scale rates and the consequences of inequality are being masked by the willingness of social workers to provide financial aid directly to those unable to manage on the resources allocated to them. If social workers refused to assist cases where the problem was one of poverty then the real issue would be highlighted and the consequences of inequality would be seen to be unacceptable. The genuine difficulty facing many social workers, no doubt, is that while they have the power to give financial aid themselves, carrying this strategy through may mean that they would have to refuse to help many whom they believe to be in need, and many who will suffer (in the short term at least) if help is not given.

A case study

The criticisms of the SBC noted above are by now accepted as valid by many social workers. However, as yet there is little hard evidence by which they can be judged. In an attempt to improve this position we undertook a study of practice in one Scottish social work department.[21] The study was based on information collected, in large measure, from written records: we are aware of the problems associated with using such records. However, in this authority at least they provided a remarkably comprehensive picture over a long period of time (approximately five years) and enabled us to amass far more information than would have been possible by any other strategy.

More specifically we examined all the records kept by two areas of the department (there were four areas in all) covering the period January 1970 to October 1975. As a result, in total over 750 cases were looked at. Whenever an application was made for financial aid the social worker was required to complete a four page form giving a wealth of personal and case information. We believe that in practice such forms were not completed unless a 'serious' application was to be made: usually, though not always, this meant that the application had the support of the social worker dealing with the case. The information collected therefore should be seen primarily as that dealing with recipients of financial aid rather than all possible applicants. The forms themselves, in general, were remarkably well completed and seem to have been taken more seriously than is often the case in such circumstances. We cannot review all of the information collected here: the attempt will be to discuss that evidence believed to be relevant to the above argument.

Table 8 shows the reasons why application for financial aid was made. The total number of reasons noted (922) is higher than the total number of clients (775) because about a quarter of clients presented more than one problem. It can be seen from this table that the bulk of applications (69 per cent) referred to problems with fuel debts; rent arrears (24 per cent) were the second most frequent problem. This pattern is similar (although fuel payments are rather higher) to that for the early 1970s for Scotland as a whole.

Table 8 **Reasons for application for financial aid**

	Number	%
Gas debt	62	6
Electricity arrears	543	59
Electricity deposit	36	4
Rent arrears	217	24
Other	64	7
Total	922	100

Table 9 shows the source of referral of the client. From this table it appears as if the bulk of clients were self referred (69·3 per cent): only a small percentage were continuing clients or referred by another agency. Two points might be made about this observation. First, this suggests that most clients approached the department purely for financial aid; aid was not given as part of continuing

Table 9 Source of referral of client

Source of referral	Number	%
Continuing	46	6·0
Client	537	69·3
Housing department	2	0*
Other local authority department	9	1·2
Hospital social worker	25	3·3
Councillor	9	1·2
DHSS	38	4·9
Other	109	14·1
Total	775	100·0

*less than 0·05

casework. Further it might be noted that over 60 per cent of the clients had never been in contact with the department on a previous occasion and that of those who had previously been in contact 42 per cent had only been in contact for financial or material aid. Thus the impression is created of clients approaching the department for financial help who would never have been in contact if such a facility had not been available. The second point to be commented on concerns the high level of self referral. This implies two things: first, a considerable knowledge by the client of the powers of the social work department to give financial aid and second, a low level of referral by other agencies, in particular the DHSS. We have other evidence to support the first of these statements. In one authority we were told that clients had heard 'through the grapevine' of a new method of considering financial aid claims by a committee of social workers: clients would frequently come into the office and ask if they were 'in time' to put in a claim to be considered by the committee. However, the second statement needs to be treated with some caution for there is the suspicion that some clients may have said they were self referred rather than referred by another agency because they did not want to give the impression of 'shopping around'. It is quite probable that many had been sent to the department by the fuel board, the housing department or a Supplementary Benefits Commission office.

A number of details of the personal position of clients might be worth recording. The majority of clients had children under school leaving age (79 per cent) and half of all clients had one child under five years old; a significant minority (36 per cent) were members of single parent families. The majority of clients were under 40 years old and about 35 per cent were under 30 years old; however, there was also a significant proportion of retired people, about 12 per cent (this group would not normally be covered by the 1963 Act, only by the 1968 Act). Only a minority of heads of household or spouses were in full time employment (about 20 per cent) with the result that few relied on earned income; the majority (about 70 per cent) were in receipt of payments from the Supplementary Benefits Commission.

Before proceeding with the claim the social worker of first contact with the client usually approached another agency to see if help was available from another source (they failed to do so in only 20 per cent of the cases). The DHSS was most frequently contacted (in almost 40 per cent of the cases), followed by the fuel and housing authorities (together in about 40 per cent of the cases). The approaches to the fuel and housing authorities seemed to find most success (a debt delay was arranged in about 30 per cent of the cases) whereas little help was forthcoming from the DHSS (financial aid was provided by them in only about 10 per cent of the cases).

However, possibly the most interesting information produced from the survey dealt with the level of income of clients and the social worker's assessment of their position. Table 10 shows the income of clients and Table 11 relates this income to Supplementary Benefit assessed subsistence levels. From Table 10 it can be seen that about 60 per cent had incomes totalling less than £30 a week

Table 10   Total incomes of clients' families

£	Number	%
Less than 10	14	2
10-19·9	205	26
20-29·9	295	38
30-39·9	180	23
40-49·9	53	7
50+	28	4
Total	775	100

Note: All incomes have been adjusted to December 1975 values and over 80 per cent had incomes totalling less than £40 a week. However, the information presented in Table 11 is possibly more crucial, for this shows the relationship between the incomes of families and the December 1975 Supplementary Benefit levels. In total about 60 per cent had incomes less than basic Supplementary Benefit levels and more than 85 per cent had incomes less than Supplementary Benefit levels plus 20 per cent (a figure frequently used by researchers in this area as Supplementary Benefit entitlement as it includes an allowance for rent and special payments—in fact some researchers have used even higher figures).

Table 11   Income and Supplementary Benefit levels

	Number	%
Less than Supplementary Benefit level	476	61
Less than Supplementary Benefit level + 20%	667	86
Less than Supplementary Benefit level + 40%	723	93
Over Supplementary Benefit level + 40%	52	7

Note: Both incomes and SBC levels have been adjusted to December 1975 values

The figures produced in Table 11 may seem surprising, especially when it is remembered that about 70 per cent of these clients were in receipt of Supplementary Benefits payments. A number of possible answers might be considered. First, more clients than expected might have been below Supplementary Benefits level because the calculations were based on the December 1975 level which was a high point in the Supplementary Benefit rate cycle (rates had been increased in November 1975). In this context it is worth noting that when individual instances were examined the bulk of those below Supplementary Benefit level were very marginal cases. Second, there may have been a fairly high proportion of 'wage-stop'[22] cases and the like, particularly as the city examined had a comparatively low wage structure. Third, there may have been some miscalculation or misreporting either accidental or deliberate. In the former category one might consider the case of the Supplementary Benefits rent allowance which may not have been treated as income by clients.

However, as will be noted shortly, one other admittedly small scale survey produced very similar results, and whatever explanations are offered or caveats added it is difficult to escape the conclusion that the kinds of client dealt with had very low incomes, often as low as or lower than the present subsistence level. More generally, this

41

evidence suggests that the type of client dealt with was living on a marginal income and would always find it difficult to manage.

A distinction is sometimes drawn between a problem involving financial management and a problem involving the adequacy of the level of financial support. The distinction is not watertight but it is based on the belief that clients in the former category need the support of a social worker to help them manage their own affairs whereas clients in the latter category merely need higher incomes. It would be too extreme to say that no matter what their incomes clients in the former category would have financial problems, but it would express the spirit of this assumption to say that such clients would be unable to manage with what most other clients would consider an 'adequate' income. It is recognized that such assumptions and distinctions cause many difficulties and are far more complex than presented here, but they have been used by both the Supplementary Benefits Commission and social services departments as a rough guide to the appropriate agency for clients with financial problems to approach: clients with management problems should approach the social services department while clients with inadequate incomes should approach the SBC.

On this basis it is interesting to note that the social workers in the department we were looking at suggested that the problems faced by clients might be described as 'financial management' in only 14 per cent of the cases where financial aid was given.

It is also worth while noting the social workers' assessment of the kind of aid needed. Social workers recommended that financial aid should be given in the vast majority of cases: in fact, such aid was given in over 80 per cent of all cases. However, social workers only recommended that other non financial social work assistance should be given in a minority of cases: in fact such aid was only given in 20 per cent of all cases.

Of course, there are many reasons why social workers might not recommend non-financial aid: it does not mean that in all of these cases financial adequacy was the only problem. It might be that social workers did not recommend other aid because they knew that to do so would be futile: such aid would not be available in the department. Alternatively it might be that to give such aid would only add to what the social worker believed was an already heavy caseload of his/her own. Nevertheless, it is clear that in few instances was financial aid given as part of more general casework. In most instances it was given as an unsupervised cash handout by an overworked social worker to a client who he or she believed would manage better if merely given more financial assistance.

The picture that we are painting then, of financial aid in this authority, is of help being given to clients who (in most cases) had no previous contact with the social work department and were not assessed to be in need of 'casework assistance' when they were interviewed by social workers. They had very low incomes and in most cases their problems seemed to be caused by inadequate incomes rather than mismanagement. Many came from social groups (single parent families,[23] large families[24]) who have been identified elsewhere as facing major income maintenance problems. Finally, many were given financial aid after the social worker had approached the Supplementary Benefits Commission and the fuel and housing authorities, all of whom said that they were unwilling or unable to help.

Additional evidence

One of the drawbacks of using a case study is that one cannot necessarily generalize and talk about nationwide patterns. We are well aware (and this will be discussed later in detail) of the major differences in practice between areas over financial aid. We are also aware that some departments give financial aid largely if not exclusively in conjunction with extended social work service with their clients. However while there are no directly comparable studies of other areas some research has been carried out which broadly confirms our findings.

Thus, Heywood and Allen[25] carried out a survey of financial aid in three English and one Welsh local authority in the late 1960s. Although the study was completed before the main explosion in the use of financial aid by social services and social work departments and it only covered a small sample of clients (sixty-five in all) the information gained broadly confirms our findings. In particular it is worth while noting the large percentage of single parent families (32 per cent), the low level of income (60 per cent were on or below short term Supplementary Benefit level) and the number who were not in full time employment (over 60 per cent) and in receipt of state benefit (63 per cent).

The paper produced by a research team working from the London Borough of Tower Hamlets[26] examined payments made to clients by the Social Services Department in the early 1970s. Information was produced on 928 families and although the absence of income data was a major drawback, the other statistics produced confirm our own findings. For example, 62 per cent of all families relied totally on state benefits as their source of income, and a large number (in fact a surprisingly high proportion), 62 per cent were categorized as 'lone parents'. In the majority of cases another agency was approached to help before financial assistance was given directly; in

54 per cent of the cases the DHSS was approached, but the DHSS only offered help in 4 per cent of the cases.

There are, in addition, a number of other studies which have produced evidence on the percentage of clients in receipt of financial aid from social work departments who are also clients of the SBC. Thus Hawker and Emmett[27] in their study of twelve London boroughs found that in eight, more than 40 per cent of clients given financial aid were in receipt of Supplementary Benefit. Similarly, in surveys in Edinburgh, Clackmannanshire and one area of Glasgow the percentages recorded were 75, 55 and 84 respectively.[28]

Conclusion

It is impossible, from the evidence available, to satisfy all of the arguments about the boundary problems between the SBC and social services and social work departments. In particular, Jordan's assertion that the SBC has deliberately reduced the scope of its service to clients, is difficult to determine. One would need a much more detailed study of the operation of the SBC, of the extent of the centralization of its operations and of the problems caused by such centralization to be able to offer a balanced assessment. His arguments are well presented and are an important part of the debate but are by no means unchallenged.[29] It is possible that social services and social work departments have taken over more responsibility for income maintenance not only because of the policy of the SBC but also because of failures on the part of social work. Maybe social work has taken over responsibility for income maintenance because it has never had a clear and precise idea about the way that financial aid through social work should be used.. Further, in a subsequent chapter we shall point to major differences in the way financial aid through social work has been used between local authorities. If social work has taken over more income maintenance functions simply because of the policy of the SBC, then why do these variations exist? Are they the result of variations in SBC policy or variations in need, or are they at least partly the result of variations in the policy of social services and social work departments?

Nevertheless, although at this stage one cannot apportion 'blame' there is now a considerable body of evidence available to suggest that the bulk of financial aid given through social work has been directed to clients who, if the powers given under Section 1 of the 1963 Act and Sections 12 and 24 of the 1968 Act had not existed, might have sought and been given help by the Supplementary Benefits Commission. If this is the case then what are the consequences?

Clearly there are consequences for the SBC. It may well relieve them of some pressure and of the need to exercise discretion to the extent that has occurred in the past. The evidence suggests that certain policy makers might welcome such a trend. It also enables the SBC to centralize its organization to a greater degree, possibly to effect economies of scale and it may be claimed, as a result, introduce a more efficient service.

There are also consequences for social workers and social work departments. Some have argued that the demands for financial aid currently being placed on social workers are stopping them making more imaginative use of the powers given. Thus, specifically referring to Scotland, it has been said:[30]

> Section 12 of the Social Work (Scotland) Act 1968 is an imaginative piece of legislation which enables local authorities to spend money 'to promote social welfare'. Very few projects which utilise the great scope of this provision have been inaugurated, largely because scarce staff resources and money have been tied up in the more pressing problem of dealing with families whose vital life support systems (electricity, gas, shelter) will be withdrawn if financial help is not given urgently.

Others have pointed to the way in which the need to deal with large numbers of financial aid cases is hampering other work:[31]

> Social workers in local authorities are being prevented from carrying out their functions with regard to the care of the elderly, disabled and children by demands made upon their services by claimants of the Supplementary Benefits Commission. Social work departments in Scotland are dangerously understaffed at present and these additional tasks undertaken by Social Workers are undermining their ability to provide services to Children's Panels, Courts and the many other duties placed on them by the Social Work (Scotland) Act 1968.

One of the ways of dealing with these problems may be to separate social workers from some of the more routine aspects of financial aid. This was tried in Glasgow through the use of what was termed the 'Financial Assistance Group'. This group consisted of a body of trained clerical staff who were given the power to deal with routine cases of financial assistance (they could deal with amounts not exceeding £20 per client themselves) for fuel and rent arrears. Social workers were only called in if the client specifically requested help or the case was a particularly involved one. The scheme had the advantage that it freed social workers from routine work and allowed them to concentrate on more imaginative and promotional aspects of their task. However, it might be argued that it achieved little more than transferring a Supplementary Benefits function to the local authority and the particular scheme described has been modified since regionalization.

The development of financial aid through social work also has consequences for clients. Earlier it was noted that some social workers believed that they were better suited, because of their training, to exercise discretion. However, there are drawbacks to the exercise of discretion by social workers from the client's point of view. First, discretion is usually exercised without recourse to a body of rules: as a result a client may not be certain that an application for aid will be dealt with in the same way by every social worker. Second, the social worker's discretion is not tempered by the ability of the client to obtain a 'second opinion' or appeal to an independent body; the decision of the social worker is final. Third, the client will probably not be given a reason by the social worker for his decision on a claim for financial aid and there is no source to which the client can look for information about how the social worker should act. These disadvantages are emphasized in the following quotation from the National Federation of Claimants' Union's Handbook:[32]

> The Social Services Department, that's the Welfare, has the power to pay your gas or electricity bill or your rent arrears if otherwise your children would have to go into care, but the welfare are even worse than Social Security—they ask you all sorts of questions about your private life and when they refuse to pay you there is no right of appeal.

Housing departments and fuel authorities

In many authorities a large proportion of financial aid through social work is given to assist with rent arrears. In Scotland overall the figure is around 50 per cent: in one of the authorities examined by Heywood and Allen over 50 per cent of aid was given to deal with rent and rate arrears and in the study of Tower Hamlets[33] it was shown that in 1971-2 40 per cent of aid was given to deal with housing problems. Studies of London boroughs[34] have shown that in general little aid has been given specifically to deal with rent arrears but a great deal of aid has been given to provide bed and breakfast accommodation and it can be argued that both rent arrears and bed and breakfast payments indicate a housing problem.

The housing problems that give rise to the need for financial aid or bed and breakfast accommodation have a number of different sources. One source, especially in urban areas, may relate to the adequacy of the housing stock. There may simply be a shortage of adequate housing, or a shortage in specific sectors (in particular the low cost renting sector). The need to provide bed and breakfast accommodation is often directly related to the housing shortage. Another source may be the policy of the public sector housing authority (usually the local authority, but in some areas it may be the New Town Housing Corporation and in Scotland it may be the Scottish Special Housing Association) towards eviction. In some areas the housing authority will accept responsibility for 'homelessness'. We discussed the impact of such an acceptance with one social work department and were told that almost overnight it had eliminated the need to provide financial aid to cover rent arrears: moves have recently been made in Britain on a national basis to compel local authority housing departments to accept responsibility for homelessness. A further source of problems may be the rent collection policy of the housing agency. Less frequent collections or a change from door-to-door to office rent collection often creates problems for people on low incomes who find it difficult to budget. For this reason a recent Government committee has recommended that 'changes to less frequent collection and to office collection rather than door-to-door should only be made with great caution'.[35] In some cases the real source of the housing problem is the level of income. It may be either that the level of income is insufficient to provide funds to purchase satisfactory housing in a high cost area or that failure to pay rent regularly is simply an indication of poverty. Finally, the source of housing problems may be inadequate budgeting on the part of the client, or what are sometimes called management problems.

Of course the difference sources of housing problems are not mutually exclusive: one may cause the other and frequently more than one source may affect the same client group. It is also difficult to assess with confidence the relative importance of the different sources. A number of studies of rent arrears[36] have concluded that poverty is the chief cause of problems but they cannot be considered to have foreclosed argument on the issue completely.

Rent arrears clearly present both housing authorities and social service or social work departments with a major dilemma. The housing authority is frequently under public pressure to keep its housing account 'in good order'. This demand includes dealing sternly with rent defaulters. The argument can be made in terms of reducing the burden that arrears place on ratepayers or setting a 'good example' for other tenants. There is also little doubt that some housing department officials become exasperated by the frequency with which certain tenants seem to reappear as 'problem cases' and, of course, it is frequently charged that they develop a bureaucratic and impersonal attitude towards such cases.

There is little doubt that social service and social work departments, in some areas, merely reap the repercussions of the actions of the housing department. If a housing department evicts a family for non payment of rent it may reduce its problem of rent arrears but increase the problems with which the social services department has to deal. Social workers cannot idly stand by and watch children be 'put on the street'.

Recently attempts have been made to increase the co-ordination between the housing and social services or social work departments, and so avoid action which does not solve problems but merely transfers them from one public agency to another. Thus, the Morris Committee[37] argued for greater co-operation and co-ordination between social work and housing departments; specifically it recommended that headquarters officials of housing departments and area social work officials should meet regularly to discuss rent arrears.

Fuel and housing debts vie with each other for the dubious distinction of being the most important cause of the need for financial aid through social work. In recent years in some areas fuel debts seem to have been winning the battle: in Scotland they have sometimes accounted for 40 per cent of all financial aid and in many English authorities the proportion is as high, if not higher. Some of the reasons for the increasing number of fuel debts have already been referred to: principally the rising cost of fuel.

In more general terms the source of many fuel debts has much in common with the source of many housing problems. For example, they may simply be related to inadequate income, or the method of payment (the reduction in the number of pre payment meters and the lengthening of periods between bills are thought to cause major problems) or they may be related to the budgeting problems of clients. They may also be related to specific developments in housing; here reference is being made to the increasing number of local authority housing estates where central heating has been installed in accommodation.

Again, as with housing problems, the sources of fuel debts are not mutually exclusive and frequently overlap, and it is difficult to evaluate their relative importance. In the same way, though, it can be argued that by cutting off supplies the fuel authority is merely transferring a problem from one public body to another and it is difficult to see how, even if the source of the problem is mismanagement, such action can make it any easier to find a solution. Possibly more attention has been paid to co-ordination between fuel and social work authorities than it has between housing and social work authorities. In many areas liaison agreements have been worked out and these have been encouraged following meetings between national representatives.[38] Yet, the national agreements seem to have done little more than spell out the ability of the social work department to give aid, and the local liaison arrangements are patchy in their effectiveness.

Both rent and fuel debts present major problems for a variety of public agencies. The housing departments and fuel authorities feel that they have to operate on a sound economic footing (in the case of the latter bodies they refer to the commercial obligations imposed on them by Parliament) while the social services and social work departments complain that they are merely having to deal with the problems created by other public agencies. The social services and social work departments also fear that the more they deal with the problems presented the more the other public bodies will adapt their policies to take account of this and the less willing they will be to offer help themselves.

Co-ordination is often said to be the answer to such problems. Certainly better co-ordination can do little harm, yet it may not solve the problem. If the problem is not merely technical or management based, but related to poverty, then better co-ordination will be only of marginal assistance. It might be argued that if the problem is one of poverty then neither the housing departments nor the fuel authorities on the one hand or the social services or social work departments on the other, should be given the responsibility for finding a solution. As when we discussed the relationship between social work and the SBC, it might be argued that the more they do so, the more they obscure the real problem and prevent agitation for its solution.

Chapter four

Social work and assistance services: comparative experience

In Britain although social workers have the power to offer financial aid to clients there is still a clear division between social work and assistance agencies. The same is not true in all other countries. For example, in the USA and in a number of European countries social workers are employed by, and social work is undertaken from within, assistance organizations.

In this chapter we will look centrally at the way social work and assistance services have been integrated in the USA. Attention will be concentrated on the Aid for Families with Dependent Children programme, one of the major and most contentious of American social security provisions. This attention can be justified on a number of grounds, but possibly most importantly because of the extent to which the American experience with social work and social assistance has influenced attitudes in Britain. Olive Stevenson has commented, 'as in many other aspects of British social work, British attitudes and feelings, especially among social scientists and young social workers, are coloured by some knowledge, directly or indirectly, of the American experience of public assistance'.[1]

In our discussions on the American scene we will make reference to European experience. This is particularly interesting because a number of European countries have integrated social work and social assistance much more than in Britain, but without the extent of the problems faced in America.

The USA. 'Aid for Families with Dependent Children'

The American social security system was established in 1935 as part of President Roosevelt's New Deal response to the great depression. Contributory benefits cover the regularly employed for retirement,

50

unemployment and for the death of the breadwinner. Under the same Social Security Act, the federal government intervened for the first time in non-contributory public assistance, which had previously been the responsibility of states and local authorities. The federal government contributed 50 per cent of assistance costs provided certain general standards were complied with. These included the right of appeal and a 'fair hearing' for any applicant declared ineligible, the application of uniform standards throughout the state, and the provision of assistance in cash rather than kind or vouchers. In contrast to the British Poor Law tradition of a service intended to be a comprehensive safety net for all destitute persons irrespective of the reasons for their inability to support themselves, the USA's programmes were intended as a complement to the insurance services, offering coverage to particular needy groups which could easily be categorized but which could not be assimilated in any scheme where benefits had to be strictly earned through past contributions. Poor people who did not fall into any defined category, or who were declared ineligible under a state rule had to rely on local 'general assistance' which remained entirely a state and local government responsibility.

The assistance programmes initiated in 1935 were Old Age Assistance (necessary for the elderly who had not had time to build up pension rights); Assistance for the Blind; Aid to the Permanently and Totally Disabled and Aid to Dependent Children. Aid to Dependent Children was a service for children, not in residential care, whose fathers were dead or incapacitated but who were not covered by social insurance provisions. Later the programme was expanded to provide benefits for the mothers and other caretakers responsible for children, and since 1961 it has been possible to include families where the father is at home but unemployed, although when it was introduced only about half the states took up this option.

Aid for Families with Dependent Children (AFDC) has been the most contentious part of income maintenance in the USA and is the only one of the programmes in which serious efforts have been made to supply social work, known confusingly as 'social services', to recipient families. It has been a very large programme; in the 1960s about 4 per cent of children in the USA were receiving allowances and as there are no family allowances it has been the main cash service directed to children. To be eligible a family has to be needy, but because need is defined as the gap between family income and the cost of living essentials, and the cost of living essentials are laid down by the state, what is accepted as need varies from state to state. It should also be noted that some states have maximum grants, so that some larger families have received less than their assessed needs.

In 1935, it was expected that most beneficiaries would be widows' children, but by the 1940s it was apparent to the public that the programme was overwhelmingly serving the children of unmarried mothers and those whose fathers had deserted. Politicians and public had far less sympathy for these groups, and critics complained that the programme was an encouragement to immorality, encouraging fathers to desert their responsibilities and unmarried women to bear children. During and after the war, many poor people migrated to urban centres where they were unable to rely on the traditional support systems they had known in rural areas, particularly the South, and in the 1950s and 1960s welfare rolls expanded dramatically. In the later years, further pressure was put on the programme when the welfare rights movement encouraged claims and challenged state eligibility rules.

The programme had to contend with public hostility at both congressional and state levels and with legislative and administrative impedimenta. In 1950, Congress passed a 'Notice to Law Enforcement Officers' amendment, precluding federal contributions in cases where fathers had deserted, unless the state public assistance agency reported the missing parent to appropriate law enforcement officers with a view to the father being charged with his legal obligations. This made the welfare agencies put pressure on mothers to reveal information and to declare ineligible those who would not or could not co-operate. Of even greater importance in restricting benefits and coercing behaviour were 'suitable home' rules and 'man in the house' rules introduced by many states in attempts to restrict expenditure.

About half the states restricted entry to the programme by requiring the home in which the child was living to be a suitable environment for child rearing. These rules were initially described as a method of making the agency responsible for children's welfare, but in some jurisdictions they were used chiefly to control and sanction the behaviour of mothers. A mother applying for aid might have to sign an undertaking such as the following:[2]

> I do hereby promise and agree that until such time as the following agreement is rescinded, I will not have any male callers coming to my home nor meeting me elsewhere under improper conditions. I also agree to raise my children to the best of my ability and will not knowingly contribute or be a contributory factor to their being harmed by my conduct. I understand that should I violate this agreement the children will be taken from me.

While a home might be considered unsuitable because of neglect, abuse or exploitation of children, very few claims were excluded on these grounds. States which enacted these rules used them almost exclusively to declare families ineligible on the grounds of mothers having had children out of wedlock. These pressures had their main effect on Negro families. Those who were cut off were sometimes eligible for 'general assistance', but in many areas no public relief was available to them.[3] In 1960, Louisiana enacted a rule which cut nearly 30,000 mothers off the AFDC roll, because the women had given birth to illegitimate children after going on relief. The law was retroactive and was applied to many families where there had not been any birth for several years. This caused a national scandal. The federal commissioner for social security ruled, however, that the existence of a 'suitable home' rule could not exclude a state from receiving federal funds for its AFDC programme, even though these rules often resulted in states leaving children in homes they considered unsuitable, but declining to supply their subsistence needs.[4] The federal government sought to remedy this anomaly by refusing to contribute in respect of any child living in home conditions which had been declared unsuitable. This did not entirely solve the problem of hostile and discriminating administration; in some states the mothers considered morally reprehensible were discouraged from applying for AFDC, for example by threats of prosecution for child neglect.[5]

The other version of the policy of restriction was 'man in the house' or 'suitable father' rules. A number of states interpreted the Social Security Act in such a way that even a casual relationship between a mother and a man was taken to mean that her children had two able-bodied parents and were not 'needy' or 'dependent' under the terms of the act. It did not matter if the man in question had no legal obligations to support the children or any income with which to do so. Like the 'suitable home' rules these provisions were found chiefly in the Southern states and aimed at Negro claimants. Some rules insisted that the father must be continually absent from the home, and this prevented the genuinely separated or divorced father from visiting his children in case this should deprive them of support. Among methods of gaining evidence of a man in the house were midnight searches and reliance on often flimsy circumstantial evidence. The Supreme Court eventually modified the effect of these rules, by declaring midnight searches illegal and defining men who could be counted as fathers under the Act as men who had a legal duty to support the children.

In 1967 and 1971, important attempts were made to alter policy regarding needy and dependent children. The Work Incentive Program and the Family Assistance Plan were intended to reduce drastically the number of families eligible for aid and required mothers to register for work or training. There were monetary incentives for those who participated and greatly reduced benefits for those who refused to take part. Under FAP, a programme of day centres for children was to be initiated, but lack of these facilities would not be good cause for non-participation if the state agency decided that suitable arrangements for care could be made.

This sketch of the AFDC programme has necessarily been brief and general as its main aim has been to provide a background for the discussion of the role of social work in an assistance scheme. Considerable emphasis has been placed on the restrictive nature of the programme, and certainly this has been its most widely discussed feature. However, it should be stressed that while the programme clearly has had restrictive features and overtones, there have been major differences in implementation between states. In some states restriction has been at a minimum: possibly only in Southern states has it been at a maximum.

Although the Social Security Act of 1935 did not refer to any other services besides income support, the programme from the beginning was influenced by social workers' ideas. The federal guidelines were drawn up by people involved in social work, who feared both the impersonality of mass relief and the hostility of many local communities to their poorer citizens. Federal state manuals reflected the belief 'that talking problems out with an accepting non-judgmental, knowledgeable person helped ease tensions and promote problem solving'.[6] The programme came to be regarded as part of social work and its caseworkers were generally regarded as social workers, though few of them were qualified. In many states, caseworkers were expected to give advice and assistance on employment, health, legal matters and general family problems.

In 1956 and 1962 the federal legislation was amended to improve 'social services' in the programme. Based on the hope that increased concern with the personal problems of dependent families would reduce the numbers needing assistance, states were authorized to furnish 'rehabilitation and other services' to AFDC families 'to help maintain and strengthen family life' and to help them to 'attain or retain capability for maximum self support and personal independence'. The federal grant was increased to 75 per cent of costs where services were given to cases in the following defined categories: unmarried mothers, older children with potential for self support, deserted families and children with special problems. A case plan had to be made for each case and 'social service', defined as a contact, usually at the client's home, at least every three months, had to be given. Federal funds were also given for social work education for public assistance employees.

There was, of course, great variation across the USA in the way AFDC workers integrated social work with income maintenance. In some areas caseworkers were no more than public assistance officials and used their responsibility to give 'services' to harass clients and to look for 'offences' under state rules. In many states, however, these social workers were anxious to provide a useful service to their clients.

Keith-Lucas, who researched in two Southern agencies, suggests that caseworkers looked on the relationship between cash giving and social work in one of three ways. First, some saw cash giving as a purely mechanical task, quite separate from the 'services' which seemed to them to be the essence of their work. Second, others considered cash giving as 'a tool in the treatment of social ills, to be more or less manipulated by the worker for the clients' interests or betterment.[7] Such workers operated with a notion of 'adjustment', based on their own opinions of what socially approved behaviour should be and saw it as their responsibility to try to change clients accordingly'.[8] A third group saw cash giving itself as a social work activity. They believed that 'to help a person obtain his rights, to express his needs, and to choose whether or not to accept the program offered by the agency is not a simple clerical operation, but demands professional skill'.[9]

Social work services were offered throughout the AFDC programme. A client asking for help was the subject of an eligibility study. This meant that his or her income and needs were assessed and a programme of action was drawn up. It was believed that such tasks, because of their complex nature, should only be undertaken by professional personnel. For example, in the eligibility study a mother often had to provide a great deal of documentary evidence, including children's birth certificates and evidence of residence in the state. It was the caseworker's job to help her obtain these. Similarly the caseworker was expected to relieve the client's assumed distress about applying for assistance and to help with conflicts which arose from this. Again the decision whether or not to enter the programme was considered to be one with which the client would need help. There might be several possibilities including finding a job with day care facilities for the children and applying for 'general assistance' which offered a quick decision but lower grants. The application process has been described as a way of enhancing a person's decision making abilities.[10] Lastly, those applicants who were not eligible had to be helped appropriately; for example, they might be referred for 'general assistance'.

A client who was accepted by AFDC was assumed by those who advocated the social work approach to be likely to have problems including not only the psychological effects of financial need, but also a range of other difficulties. 'Members of such families feel less adequate, more vulnerable, more submissive than others; they lose their sense of self-esteem and self-respect. Some feel a sense of isolation from others, a fear of rejection as "free loaders, welfare chisellers". Many such families live on the fringes of society, reflecting society's contempt for and rejection of them.'[11] Kadushin lists a number of studies which show that a high proportion of AFDC families had multiple problems warranting psychiatric or intensive casework help and needed guidance in caring for the emotional needs of their children.[12] The fact that these problems are not confined to AFDC families was not seen as a reason for not giving them services. The programme was sometimes seen as an elite rehabilitive service, accepting only deserving clients, promoting their enhanced social functioning, improving their child care and encouraging their self support.

The usual service method was through individual casework. This 'traditional' approach was retained partly because federal audits and grants were on a case basis and the amendments of 1962 required case visits. Group methods have also been used, both at the 'eligibility' stage to present information and in ongoing cases for discussion of common problems such as rearing a child in a fatherless family and social activities for single women. 'During such group meetings of these various kinds,' writes Kadushin, 'clients have shared information that they had not previously disclosed to their caseworker and agency staff members have been given an opportunity of gaining additional understanding of their clients.'[13]

Handler and Hollingsworth's work *The Deserving Poor* provides an account of how 'social services' were actually delivered in one AFDC agency and how they were perceived by clients. It was emphasized that this was a department with a generally good reputation for meeting clients' economic needs. The authors point to the effect the very large caseloads had on any attempt to give a real individualized service. For most clients there were neither the detailed enquiries of punitive and moralistic practice nor much attempt to offer casework. Complaints from neighbours, especially if they came via the police, or some obvious family emergency might bring more attention. 'But absent something unusual, the caseworker is likely to do no more than make the minimum number of visits and fill out the prescribed forms.'[14]

Nevertheless, the great majority of recipients surveyed spoke well of their caseworkers and the agency, though they did not expect much more of them than provision of income. These friendly attitudes to caseworkers seemed related to the innocuous character of the conversations which took place in home visits. Caseworkers, for the most part, kept away from sensitive issues, such as clients' social lives, relations with men and home care or topics which might lead to complaints or requests for help which the caseworker could not provide. On the other hand, the social workers were happy to talk about health care because they could make referrals for free medical treatment, which the clients appreciated. When caseworkers expressed disapproval of their conduct, however, clients resented this and even when they admitted to being helped by advice they were likely to say that they were 'bothered or annoyed' by the discussions. 'In other words, as long as the caseworkers avoided playing a meaningful role in the lives of the clients, whether positively or negatively, they could count on clients' passiveness and, more important, overall satisfaction. Unless the caseworkers could deliver tangible goods a more meaningful intervention ran risks.'[15]

In reviewing social work within AFDC, it is important to stress that the programme operated in the context of a largely hostile public opinion, convinced that large scale fraud was taking place and, even in the more generous states, with policies which in Britain would be considered restrictive in an income maintenance programme. In their task of awarding financial grants, social workers had to compromise between their personal concerns to be generous to needs and a critical local opinion. There is good reason to think that casework staff and especially senior workers did manage to modify what in many areas would have been even 'tougher' treatment of poor families. On the positive side too, there is a suggestion that giving responsibility for confirming eligibility to someone who is known by the client to have a general concern with his well-being prompted claimants to make more requests for special grants.[16]

In attempting to be a social work agency, however, AFDC seems to have been compromised by its primary public assistance function and this was the case even in areas where allowances and eligibility conditions were relatively generous. In other social work settings, even where the client is under some pressure to participate, the interaction grows out of the client's statement of his felt needs and the sensitive caseworker responds at such a pace and in such a way that the client has a reasonable idea of what the caseworker is trying to do. In AFDC, at the first encounter 'the client was required to answer a highly structured series of questions that resembled sociological research interviews, which utilize questionnaires to generate systematic data'. In other agencies, client and worker generally determine the length of service together; in AFDC the number of meetings and period of service was controlled by agency requirements. Usually, when a client left the income maintenance programme, possibly when she 'broke a rule' and became ineligible, 'social service' ceased, even though the need for help might have been greater than ever.[17]

Considerable emphasis has been placed on the way in which the link between social work and AFDC gave social workers coercive powers. Social workers possessed considerable discretion and controlled finance and other material aid needed by the client. The control of such resources can be used as a powerful weapon to persuade clients to accept unwanted guidance and adopt a course of action which they otherwise would have seen as undesirable.

Despite attempts after 1962 to increase the number of trained social workers in AFDC only a small proportion of staff have had any relevant education. Those who were interested in social work as a career left as soon as they could for other agencies with less equivocal responsibilities and lighter caseloads. Many have argued that the development of social work in the USA has been held back because of the link between social work and assistance services. It has been suggested that social work will only be able to develop as a distinct profession once it has been freed from the ties of financial aid and the assistance services.

In the later 1960s, the social work profession engaged in serious criticism of the combination of eligibility checking with 'social service'. Politicians too reacted against 'social service' when despite increased expenditure on it, welfare rolls continued to rise. The contradictions of AFDC were clear: first, how could a worker, responsible for checking eligibility, who had to take account of great public concern to eradicate fraud, also offer a therapeutic service which had to be based on mutual trust? Second, how could a social service, directed at individual rehabilitation, achieve results when the causes of its clients' predicaments were major economic and social forces?

In 1967, the Social Security Act was amended to require that the functions of eligibility checking and social service be carried out by separate personnel. The income maintenance function is now generally carried out by 'eligibility technicians' and eligibility seems to have lost a lot of its former significance. It remains to be seen whether or not 'social services' will have an important place in future American public assistance programmes.

Discussion

The link between social work and social assistance in the USA has provoked considerable hostility. It has been argued that the link has severely hampered and distorted the development of social work as well as leading to the provision of a harsh and sometimes unjust service for clients.

In the introduction to this chapter we noted that knowledge of the American scheme, and knowledge of the criticisms made of it, have influenced social workers' ideas in this country. However, it is important to recognize the environment in which the American developments have taken place, and not simply to assume that one can use the American experience as a guide to what will happen in Britain. As Olive Stevenson has commented, 'the extrapolations from the American scheme are often inappropriate for they do not take into sufficient account the differences between the two countries, culturally, and in social policy and social work in particular'.[18]

It is especially important to recognize that in America social work and social assistance have been linked in a social security system which differed (and differs) markedly from our own. The social security system itself is far more restrictive than in Britain and far less comprehensive. It is worth while noting that the USA spends a lower proportion of its GNP on social security than any other western industrialized nation. We have emphasized the discriminatory nature of a great deal of the American social security system, particularly the AFDC programme. There is little doubt that the discrimination present in the programmes has had a major impact on the way social workers have carried out their responsibilities and one needs to be cautious in assuming that social workers with similar powers would necessarily use them in a comparable way in a country which had a different social security system and a different approach to social assistance.

In this context it is worth while noting that in a number of European countries social work and social assistance have been linked, and although the link has not been without criticism, it has not aroused anything like the controversy seen in the USA. In West Germany, for example, the social security system is dominated by the concept of *Sozialhilfe* which denotes more comprehensive support than just financial aid and includes other material benefits, residential care, and concern with claimants' general well-being. The explicit aim of *Sozialhilfe* is to rehabilitate claimants to independence and to integrate them in their communities. Although the social assistance scheme is regulated by the Federal and Land governments, the services themselves are provided by lower level social assistance agencies and local social welfare offices both provide social assistance and employ social workers. It should be stressed, though, that while social workers are employed by assistance giving agencies they are not directly involved in the assessment or checking of claims by clients.

In France, though, even this division is absent and social security and social work are even more closely linked. The social security system is, as in Germany, simply regulated by the national government, while the main burden of operation is carried by a variety of local semi-public bodies, managed by boards of elected representatives. Throughout social security agencies in France, social assistance and social work are closely linked, although the link is possibly best seen in the family welfare agencies.

The European examples do not mean, of course, that social assistance and social work should be linked, any more than the American experience meant that they should not be linked. Social assistance and social work have been linked and have operated in France and Germany in a distinct context. For example, they have operated in a system of social services where local operation and responsibility have long been accepted. The bodies operating the systems largely are locally controlled and elected and assistance rates are locally determined: in Germany assistance rates are fixed by reference to a national basket of goods but are based on regional price levels. The link between social work and social assistance is also part of a long tradition. In France the social security agencies developed out of mutual aid organizations and inherited from them a concern for general social welfare. Further, in Germany in particular, social insurance has been developed to take over a much more significant role than in Britain, with the result that a much smaller proportion of the population claims assistance: for example, less than 3 per cent of the elderly claim assistance in Germany.

It might well be argued, of course, that it is only since the Second World War that Britain's social security system has developed in a radically different fashion to that of its European neighbours. Certainly the pre 1948 British system was closer to that of many European countries than it is today and it may well be suggested that a return to locally based assistance services is possible. While this may be true it does not detract from the need to view any link between social work and social assistance in its particular context and to assess the extent to which the comments about the link, whether positive or negative, are dependent on a particular environment.

Conclusions

Comparative study can be useful and stimulating: even a cursory look at social services and forms of social work abroad can stimulate the case for development of our own services and, provided we think through the effects they might have on other aspects of our services, their comparative costs and their probable effects on clients' problems, some diffusion of ideas can be fruitful. This is particularly so in the case of financial aid and social work. It is instructive to remember that the divisions maintained in Britain are not adhered to elsewhere and to consider the consequences of alternative strategies.

References to what is happening in social services overseas appear occasionally in the press, and the American experience is covered by a good deal of social work literature. Few have suggested that Britain should follow the American model: rather it has been shown to illustrate the dangers inherent in a particular approach to the social services. In the coming years, though, we are likely to see more attempts to persuade Britain to adopt a European model. These attempts may be made by people who believe this European model to be superior, as well as by people who believe that a greater integration of European social services is desirable. There may well be merit in striving for greater integration of social services in Europe and there may well be aspects of European social services from which Britain can learn. It is most important, though, to beware of superficial comparisons and evaluations based on partial accounts of schemes in other countries.

In the case of financial aid and social work, while it is important to examine the methods of operation in other countries, it is just as important to avoid hasty conclusions. The comparative evidence from America on the way social work has been integrated with social assistance no more 'proves' that the integration of social assistance and social work is undesirable than the evidence from Europe proves that it is desirable. The evidence and ideas we can gain from comparative study are important but must be treated with caution.

Chapter five

Social work practice and financial aid

The social workers who argued for the powers conferred in 1963 and 1968 wanted them not because they thought that money was usually more important than other methods of social help, but because they thought that financial aid would remove encumbrances to using other social work methods. However, although the statutes authorize payments to avoid the need for reception into care, or some greater future expenditure, for most social workers such reasons alone might not be enough to justify the involvement of qualified social work staff to dispense them. To be satisfying to social workers who aspire to distinguish a professional function, the task of allocating financial aid has to be accommodated in some general model of the purposes of social work. In this chapter we look at a number of approaches to financial aid which have been suggested in the past, not in a spirit of criticism, but to find the guidance which has been and is being offered to social workers as part of their professional education.

Early voluntary philanthropy

Material aid has a long tradition in social work which is associated particularly with the voluntary philanthropy which was systematized in Britain a century ago. Its central purpose, which shaped its methods, was to establish its clientele in economic independence and personal satisfaction. Despite a recent revival of the voluntary sector, organized philanthropy has been far less important since the establishment of state welfare services. Nevertheless, its approaches are still influential and instructive in considering a number of issues facing modern social work.

The philanthropic system was dominated by the Charity Organisation Society which was founded in 1869, to regulate charitable giving. The Society is remembered for its opposition to state social services, for its gospel of individualism and for the moralistic distinctions it made between the 'deserving' and 'undeserving', which took more account of past conduct than of present need. It cannot have enjoyed much popularity among the poor and by the 1880s, when inconsistencies between its doctrine of individualism and the realities of economic life were becoming apparent, it was very conscious of influential middle class opponents. Since the Society tried to present itself as a quasi-official organization making decisions on public relief, it faced not only criticisms of its principles, but also hostile press reports of the way particular cases were handled by its district committees.[1] As late as 1940, its administrative committee considered the charge that the COS was arrogant and dictatorial and recommended that 'Secretaries should interpret the committees' decisions to other agencies tactfully'.[2] Yet the Society was an important strand in the development of social work and over the years clarified a body of principles and practices with regard to financial aid.

One of the central precepts was that decisions in all cases should be based on investigations of the applicant's history and his means. Mary Richmond, who conceptualized the COS tradition, called her best known book *Social Diagnosis*[3] and in it she seemed to suggest that solutions to a client's problems were likely to emerge from full investigation of his needs. Where material aid was required, possible suppliers of help, such as relatives and employers, would have been identified in the investigation of the client's situation and the social workers should try to mobilize appropriate assistance from family, philanthropic persons and public agencies.

Many social workers today are reluctant to become involved in the kind of detailed investigation of a client's financial needs and means suggested by Mary Richmond when considering applications for material aid. Some claim it is not their job, others are afraid that it will interfere with more important work with clients. However, as we have argued, increasingly in Britain material aid through social work is being used as income maintenance and awarded to meet bills for necessities. In such circumstances, despite their reservations, social workers may have little option but to face up to the problems that confront any assistance agency, such as the tendency for people who feel themselves in need not to declare all their resources, and the real possibility of deceit. Assistance services often guard against these possibilities by routine doubting of clients and requiring those with unusual needs to be particularly persistent. Such procedures would be considered inimical to social work, but so long as financial aid is at least partly income maintenance, pressure will be put on social workers to discuss financial affairs with their clients fully and honestly, so that they are not arbitrary in their use of available funds.

A second principle of the COS was that the aid should only be given in cases where it would make some improvement in the recipient's position; usually, but not necessarily, in his ability to earn. This was why the Society was so concerned about 'character'. The applicant's past conduct was an indication of his future behaviour. A case in the 1920s provoked discussion of this belief. An application for an invalid tricycle was refused on the grounds that there was suspicion that the man involved had been dishonest while in the army. Was it not possible, some argued, that such a man might pawn the appliance for drink? One dissident argued that help should be given whenever it could really (and as a rule permanently) benefit the applicant and when the applicant was unable to obtain what he needed by his own efforts. When proof of these two conditions was obtained, help should be given irrespective of other circumstances, or how the person might behave in the future. However, this point of view did not prevail; the view that past behaviour was an indicator of ability to benefit from help was deeply ingrained in the Society's thinking.[4]

The issue of 'helpability' is relevant today as all social work services are in short supply and have to be rationed. Some social workers believe that they should give financial aid only in cases where money is expected to make a lasting difference of some kind which the social worker considers to be an improvement in the client's situation; for example it might be used to relieve an otherwise intractable debt problem which had clearly arisen from unwise spending in the past, but the client seemed both prepared and able to follow advice on budgeting in the future.

Allocation on the basis of the client's ability to make progress on the social worker's terms may be reasonable as a general principle, if the good sense of the caseworker is taken for granted, but it does raise problems. It excludes the possibility of giving aid to gain temporary relief in cases where no permanent change in a situation is expected. It also raises the issue of the degree to which the social work relationship is a 'contract', whereby in return for certain sorts of help, the client is expected to behave in ways suggested by the social worker. If aid is only given to those who are capable of being and willing to be helped, it gives social workers power to enforce certain kinds of behaviour.[5] It must be especially difficult to refrain from using aid in a controlling way when the need for aid arises from a debt to another official body which insists on certain standards of conduct in future, such as regular payments, and looks to the social work department to 'enforce' such behaviour. Thus if 'helpability' is a criterion, the social worker will have to clarify the extent to which the client recognizes the direction in which he is being forced to go and the 'helpful' changes in his life which are expected to occur. If the client does not recognize as actually or potentially helpful the conditions imposed, such as the rate at which the loan should be repaid, the social worker is faced with the problem of the client's right to self determination. As financial aid is nearly always given to improve the situation of families with dependants, this is particularly difficult.

A third important COS principle was that aid should only be given in the context of a friendly relationship between social worker and client. From the 1880s, its casenotes give a clear impression of continuing relationships between families (especially mothers) and the social workers.[6] In later social work theorizing the relationship was to become an essential tool of social work and a criterion of 'helpability'. A client could only be helped if a certain kind of trusting personal relationship could be formed between him and his social worker. However, many social workers today may not consider it necessary that financial aid should be given only within a social work relationship. Social workers may well perceive needs which can be met by money, but see no reason to offer a continuing association. On the other hand, the implications of money powers for the 'social work' relationship are a source of concern to many social workers. An account of practice given below[7] suggests that it is not the power to allocate money, but the way the power is used which affects the relationship, at least in terms of the client's degree of satisfaction.

COS thinking no longer dominates social work as it did in the nineteenth and early twentieth centuries. That is not to say that its principles have no continuing influence in the present day social services. More relevant to our purpose is the fact that because the Society built its work around financial aid it gave a great deal of consideration to problems similar to those which perplex modern social workers who often subscribe to very different political ideologies. Though the COS's principles may be considered anachronistic, the issues it raised are still pressing.

More recent social work theory

This is not the place for a general review of social work theory, but it is appropriate to look at the work of a number of authors who discussed the relationship between financial aid and social work. For many years psychoanalytic theory was in the ascendent in social work writing, but in the last decade other perspectives, most recently the application of systems theory, have been influential. The works we have selected span these different schools. They are by Hamilton,[8] Perlman,[9] Hollis,[10] Timms,[11] Jehu,[12] Pincus and Minnahan,[13] and

Mayer and Timms.[14] Any selection is bound to be personal and hence will attract criticism. There are many other writers who could have been included. However, we have been guided centrally in our choice by the desire to point to authors who have frequently been used in social work education. We will review what each of them has to say about financial aid and social work in turn, and then offer some comments about any general theories that may or may not emerge.

Gordon Hamilton's main work was written in the USA just after the Second World War and she makes many references to human and democratic rights, and stresses the distinction between environmental, including cultural, conditions and the individual's reaction to them. She had many links with the psychodynamic approach and although she recognized that social action might be necessary to modify unsatisfactory social conditions, she stressed the necessity of psychological knowledge in understanding the individual's perception of his situation and in helping him to cope with any difficulties in adapting to his circumstances. However, for Hamilton it was important for the individual to control his own life and make his own decisions, and she stressed that social workers should not try to impose their own standards of behaviour as a condition of providing material service. 'Concrete services and practical assistance are not contingent on conformity in behaviour. Goods and services in modern social work, as in modern medicine are given because the client has need of them.'[15]

Hamilton argued that financial need, including 'the maintenance of family life threatened by disintegration only because of loss of income', is properly the responsibility of the social security services. This is not to say that she did not recognize that a large number of recipients of public assistance need social work service in addition to money. She stressed that in order to particularize income services to individual needs, such assistance as budgeting, eliciting a person's strengths in dealing with difficulties and putting him in touch with other agencies 'is essential for rehabilitation':[16]

> Economic security while basic to a productive society is only a half way measure without individual and family responsibility and stability. Sometimes clearing up the immediate emergency by financial assistance will improve the psychological situation also; sometimes it will not, and then another formulation with the client of his problem and what he is willing to work on may be necessary.

However, Hamilton clearly distinguishes income for basic living standards, which is the responsibility of public assistance, from money used as a tool of social work. Examples of the latter are to help a client change or improve his situation, to regain his independence, to create opportunities to develop his capacities and to create special living experiences. Money grants used as treatment should favourably affect the progress of the case and constructively support ego strengths.[17]

This notion of a 'promotional' purpose distinct from meeting normal living needs is helpful in distinguishing a specifically social work function for financial aid. Yet, the potential for helping people to develop capacities is limitless, and to give social workers power to enhance individuals' opportunities could involve enormous patronage because of the power it affords to allocate special benefits to those who chance to come to the notice of social workers. To provide a holiday for a poor family might make a permanent difference to the quality of their lives, but the social worker needs some criterion for selecting particular families for this kind of help.

Florence Hollis in her text *Casework: A Psychosocial Therapy* emphasizes diagnosis (based on psychoanalytic theory) of the client's difficulties and treatment of his intra- and interpersonal conflicts. She recognizes that it is sometimes necessary to relieve environmental and material, including financial, pressures. This may be accomplished by referring the client to the public assistance agency, and the social worker may support him if he is having difficulty with the service. However, Hollis seems to recommend that this 'indirect' work be carried out by personal influence of a similar nature to the 'direct' work with clients:[18]

> Environmental work also takes place with people and through
> psychological means. We cannot physically make a landlord,
> teacher, or anyone else do something for the benefit of our
> client. We have to talk with him about it, and in the process we
> must use psychological procedures of one sort or another.
> Broadening our view of casework in this way may help us to
> narrow the distance that seems so often to separate direct
> from indirect work.

One is sceptical of the efficacy for the British local authority worker of following such advice when dealing with Supplementary Benefits or fuel board officials. Such agencies expect negotiations to be on an official to official basis and would resent any reference to their own feelings about the client and his situation.

If the social worker is in a position to provide funds directly, Hollis advises him to go fully into the implications of any grant with the client:[19]

> Often, instead of meeting the need directly, it is advisable to
> help the client bring about a change in the situation himself.

The caseworker's effort is then directed toward telling the client about possible opportunities, helping him decide whether or not he wants to use them and, if so, how to go about using them. It is preferable that a client do his own manipulation of the environment, if he can effectively do so.

The social worker should always be aware that environmental changes brought about solely for the purpose of removing unusual pressures or deficiencies do not necessarily involve an effort by the individual towards change in himself. He may function more comfortably as a result of the lifting of environmental pressure though his inner balance may remain out of equilibrium.[20] Hence the casework task is seldom completed merely by restoration of functioning through a financial grant.

Helen Harris Perlman is the chief exponent of the 'Chicago' school of casework, which focuses on the difficulties people face in solving their problems of living and coping with emotional stresses in a socially acceptable manner. She gives extensive attention to the idea of agency function; every social worker must be aware that he can only do work which is consistent with the purposes for which his agency exists. A clear conception by the caseworker of what his agency exists for and what it is able to do serves to give focus and form to what, as the client presents it, is a most complicated problem.[21] Whatever the caseworker observes as the essence of the client's problem, he is advised to give attention first to the problem as the client sees it and this may well be his immediate financial worries. Problems often arise as 'chain reactions', so, for example, difficulties in coping with financial matters may lie behind tensions in several areas of life. Though this complicates the clarification of the client's problems, it also means that a number of aspects of life which are askew may sometimes be put right by the adjustment of one.[22]

Perlman has little to say specifically about financial aid, but much of her general advice can be applied to money giving. The aim of casework is to engage the client in coping himself with his problems. The social worker works through a relationship which affects the client's emotional relation to his problems; through discussion in which the client can work out his solutions, and the provision of aid and resources which will implement the client's action on his problems. Presumably, it is preferable not to grant money until the client has clearly worked out how it is going to contribute to the solution of his problem. Yet, the social worker is reminded of his client's right to self-determination and that he must not inveigle him into consenting to any condition for a service provided.[23] This leaves the social worker in a dilemma. If the client remains convinced that a grant of money for a certain purpose is essential to solve his problems, the caseworker must either comply (if he can actually obtain funds) or deny the validity of the client's perceptions.

Perlman also reminds social workers of clients' uncertainty about the purposes of social agencies and what might be expected of them when they seek help. Clients are likely to feel an obligation to reciprocate in some way for any services rendered. Such a feeling may be less common among clients of local authority departments than of voluntary agencies, but may sometimes exist, especially where the client sees that the social worker has made a personal effort to obtain money for him.

Perlman's interest in agency function provides a link with the work of Noel Timms. Timms stresses that agencies are established to carry out broad social functions and that the worker is expected to contribute to these objectives and to clarify his own responsibilities within these purposes. He argues that specialization and clarity of purpose should be implicit in social work and he believes that they can be particularly helpful for both worker and client.

As far as material aid is concerned Timms suggests that it is up to the agency to make clear how compatible this is with its overall functions. Once this is clarified 'the caseworker's task in regard to material aid falls into line with the rest of his casework, which is aimed at answering the question, how can I help the client to use the services my agency offers?' Although Timms advises the social worker not to look on material aid 'as a necessary means of helping a family deal with its severe reality problems or establishing a relationship and thus paving the way for work on deeper problems',[24] he nevertheless recognizes that a client's request for material assistance may well be a communication which requires other or additional responses than simply granting or refusing it 'with courtesy and a mind blank to other possibilities'. For instance it might contain a message regarding his experience of being a client, or it may be a statement about some other aspect of his life. This is good advice, although many local authority social workers have the strong suspicion that many clients come to them precisely because the impression is abroad that it is a function of their departments to provide material relief. The client may have come with no motivation to express anything but his need for financial aid. As such needs are often urgent, these problems must be dealt with in some way before any other work is attempted. As Mayer and Timms suggest elsewhere the client may only communicate about other aspects of his life when he is pleasantly surprised about the way his request for material aid has been dealt with.[25]

Jehu's text seeks to apply 'learning theory' to social work. He argues that the social workers should act as therapists, seeking to eliminate the client's undesired behaviour by rewarding more acceptable actions and expressions of attitude. The ethical issues such treatment raises are discussed elsewhere in the book. Where the client is actively involved in setting goals and participating in treatment no problem is faced by the learning therapist. However, when the social worker is acting as an agent of social control and the client is under some duress, as when there is a court order involved, the responsibility for making a moral decision about acceptable methods falls largely on the social worker, although he will usually try to work together with the client in setting goals. Learning theory stresses the powerful effects of the therapist's influence in the selection of goals. 'The more effective she becomes as a behavioural technologist, the more important is her role as a moralist.'[26]

Material aid, including money, is referred to as a form of reward particularly necessary for clients who are indifferent to or distrustful of social rewards.[27] There are some cases, however, where the major factor facing a client is environmental stress and no serious behavioural change has to be worked for. In such cases, the social worker in arranging for material aid to relieve the stress should, as far as possible, avoid reinforcing maladaptive behaviour. For example, such aid should, if possible, not be given at a time when it might act as a reward for the client's aggressive or deceitful behaviour.[28]

The text by Pincus and Minnahan is based on a rather different approach. Its central aim is to show how systems theory can be applied to social work. The focus of social work should be on the interactions between people and systems in their environments which provide the material, emotional and spiritual resources required to realize their aspirations.[29] The purposes of social work are: to enhance people's problem solving and coping capabilities; to link people with systems that provide them with resources, services and opportunities; to promote the effective and humane operation of these systems and to contribute to the development and improvement of social policy. The social worker is a facilitator, helping people to use appropriate resources, and when the form the resources take frustrates people in coping with their tasks, the social worker should try to secure the adaption of the service. So, a concern with the relations between income maintenance agencies and their claimants is clearly central to the social work task, and the social worker's role includes acting as advocate for people experiencing difficulty in negotiating these systems.[30]

Pincus and Minnahan argue that social workers traditionally have been dispensers of material resources, including financial aid and have developed competences in such activities. (Unfortunately, they do not go into what these special competences are.) Further they suggest that social workers, as well as helping people in receipt of financial assistance to enhance their own coping facilities and to utilize other potential helping systems, should try to locate people who need material resources and should 'work to make their own (social workers') and other societal systems responsive to people receiving financial assistance and advocate for changes in the provision of income to poor people'.[31] This follows from Pincus and Minnahan's conception of social work as the facilitator of relations between resources and potential users, in which work for modification of policy in financial aid, as in other matters, is not an extra-curricular activity to be taken up by social workers but an integral part of the social work task.

There are several empirical studies which include discussion of the way financial aid has been associated with social work activities. Mayer and Timms, in one such study, look at clients' perceptions of the Family Welfare Association, and discuss clients' feelings about bringing material problems to a social agency and about the ways social workers treated them. They noted that often clients felt humiliated at having to ask for money and were anxious to disassociate themselves from other people who came to the Association, who they assumed were 'cadgers' and less deserving than themselves. Such clients expected that an agency dispensing material relief would treat them harshly and they thought they would be questioned severely about the ways they managed their money.

Mayer and Timms showed how the way that material problems were dealt with could have an important impact on the future progress of the case. Alternative approaches and their consequences are highlighted. First, a client's material problems might be given early consideration. Even if the extent of the material help given was less than required, nevertheless this often meant that the client was appreciative of what had been done and developed a positive attitude towards the agency. When these clients felt assured of their caseworkers' interest in them, they often gained and appreciated unexpected benefits from the relationship; they were able to unburden themselves and receive support and guidance. One less satisfactory outcome was that these clients were sometimes led by feelings of gratitude to allow the social worker to continue contact after they felt that it was no more use to them. It was especially difficult for them to break off contact when the worker was visiting them at home.

An alternative was that the material anxieties brought by clients were not dealt with early in the relationship; they frequently were dissatisfied with their treatment and gained none of the other benefits that the agency offered. In order to create a good impression they had presented themselves to the social worker in ways they felt to be humiliating. Yet the caseworker seemed to have ignored their chief concern and pressed them on seemingly irrelevant questions, such as their family relationships. They had tried to ingratiate themselves with the worker by continuing to answer his questions and behave in ways he seemed to want, so when they got no financial aid they were angry and resentful.

The authors suggest that cases where clients were satisfied followed a progression: material needs were given early consideration; once this was done, the client—not the worker—made the next move; the worker's handling of what the client presented was experienced as 'meaningful'. In cases where clients were dissatisfied, the workers ignored both the urgency and the symbolic implications of the presented material needs.

It has to be said that from the social worker's point of view, satisfied clients are not the same thing as successful cases. It would not be feasible nor probably desirable for any agency to meet all requests for material aid, even in part, in order to assure clients of the agency's concern. But consideration of Mayer and Timms's work reminds us that it is important to give priority to the client's expression of his material anxieties and to what the agency might do. If he cannot accept that the agency is unable to help him in that way, there may be little chance of doing counselling work with him, whether it be helping with relationships within the family or advice about future budgeting. It follows that social workers who know that they have little financial aid to offer should not try to steer the client away from concentrating on his material requests, but deal with them frankly though sensitively.

It is also important to remember that a client's behaviour which could appear to the social worker as demanding and manipulative may be the result of his search for actions which will impress his distress on a bureaucracy which seems uninterested. Thus the mother who threatens to leave her children at the reception desk may not be an uncaring person prepared to use her children to get her own way, but a desperate person crudely trying to fit her circumstances to the kind of situation the agency seems prepared to deal with. Her dramatic demonstration is her response to what she perceives as lack of interest in her distress either by the social work department or the agencies she has previously visited.

It is difficult to abstract any composite prescriptions about financial aid and social work from the range of writing examined. This is as much because few writers took financial aid and social work as their central theme as anything else. Most looked at this area in a subsidiary fashion; some looked at it only indirectly. Nevertheless, three very general lines of thought might be highlighted. First, it has been pointed out that although normally basic living needs for those without sufficient resources should be met by social security and assistance services, on occasions social workers may find themselves in a position to help when no other agency will. While some writers recognized dangers in social workers becoming involved in disbursing financial aid, others adopted a more positive attitude. Crucially, though, all writers recognized that at least in certain circumstances social workers would be involved in assessing and awarding financial aid. Second, it was generally stated that when social workers became involved in this practice they should give financial aid irrespective of the client's willingness to become involved in any other way, even when the client seems to have placed himself in a difficult position by his own actions. Third, it was stressed that a request or need for financial aid may indicate need for other services or the client's wish to communicate other things to the worker, such as how he feels about being a person who needs help with his problems. The social worker should be sensitive to these communications.

Social workers and financial aid—critical views

The work we have discussed above, while recognizing dangers in the misuse of financial aid, accepts that under certain circumstances it can be consistent with good social casework. Recently, a number of writers, after examining the effect of the powers in Section 1 of the Children's Act 1963, have deplored the effect of the power to give money on the social worker's ability to carry out his proper task. Broadly the argument is that the responsibility to satisfy material needs involves clients in a type of dependency which is inconsistent with a relationship in which good social work can take place.

These criticisms are cogently made by Bill Jordan, who claims that the existence of powers to supply 'hard services' including financial aid has meant that social work's clientele has been increasingly made up of people with material needs, and social casework has become of secondary importance in most departments.[32] The erosion of services provided by the Supplementary Benefits Commission, such as the closing of many local offices and the drastic reduction of visits to claimants' homes has, in places where social work has used cash-giving powers to fill apparent gaps, created a *de facto* association of social work with relief. The more social work takes on this public assistance function, the less opportunity social workers have to practise true social casework as a therapeutic relationship.

Administratively, the task of providing material aid on a large scale has resulted in a form of organization in which social workers are not only distant from important decision makers in their own agencies, but also generally unable to maintain the continuing relationships with clients which have been considered necessary for good social casework practice:[33]

> The resultant picture of a social services department is of a large organization . . . staffed by young, disaffected and relatively inexperienced workers under the close administrative control of a large hierarchy of well-organised bureaucrats and confused, alienated, senior professionals bemoaning their lack of contact with clients.

All this is to the detriment of true casework which is 'an approach to a helping relationship which is based on compassion for people in trouble, sorrow, need, sickness and various other adversities'.[34] This casework relationship is helpful to and valued by people of all economic statuses. Hence Jordan argues against any incorporation of financial aid powers into the social work agency.

Jordan's critical approach to financial aid and social work is supported by the work of Handler. He has provided an account of how workers in three children's departments used their discretionary powers to provide services which were particularly demanded by clients, such as places in children's homes and Section 1 grants.[35]

Among these desired and essential services, child care officers considered their money powers to be a special case: money has a 'runaway' quality, because so many more clients could be seen to need money than any other service; people might become dependent on regular grants to cover elementary responsibilities like fuel and rent and there seemed much more likelihood of people claiming a money grant if they heard that neighbours had had one.

The first strategy according to Handler for controlling Section 1 money was to conceal the availability of the service from clients as far as possible. For example, when one department entered into a rent guarantee with the housing authority, in order to stay an eviction order, the client would not be informed of the arrangement for fear that he would default again and expect to be helped out in the same way.

The second strategy was to attach a condition to financial aid of casework help. Many child care officers accepted the 'problem family' notion as the basis of their work. To them financial difficulties and the apparent inability to pay bills was likely to be a symptom of more general incompetence and of deep seated problems which could only be treated at the individual and family level. The difficulty which seemed most urgent to the client, for example a threatened eviction, was seen by the social worker as only a presenting problem. However, the latter sometimes used his power to forestall homelessness to strike a 'bargain' with the client who agreed to fall in with a 'casework plan'. This might be some specific action, such as a contribution to clearing arrears, or a longer lasting behaviour change, such as a promise that a member of the family would make efforts to obtain work. Not all grants were subject to conditions, especially when one payment was likely to make such a difference to a situation that the client was not likely to be in need again, and not all social workers used these 'bargains' to the same extent. However, according to Handler, use of Section 1 powers to 'enforce' casework plans on unwilling or uninterested people was a significant way in which money was associated with social work. Thus social workers were reinterpreting Section 1 as follows: 'Families seeking specific help are for the most part seeking temporary relief of symptoms of underlying, more basic problems of pathology; however, the Children's Department will only accept (that is grant the request of) those families who will accept the casework plan.' The consequence of this approach was that it 'creamed off' clients who were willing to co-operate and left the unwilling without assistance. This was justified not on grounds of necessity, but by reference to the theory of the 'problem family' and money was chiefly used as a goad or bribe to attempt to change the behaviour of 'anti-social people'.

Handler's study clearly adds weight to Jordan's claim that the powers given to social workers to offer financial aid are detrimental to the service offered to clients. The answer that can be given to Jordan's case against all financial aid powers depends on assumptions about the proper functions of social work in a public agency. Jordan's conception of social work as a therapeutic relationship offered to people in many kinds of trouble but not associated with supplying material needs represents a major challenge to historical and mainstream current thinking.

There is little doubt that some social workers will continue to press for the power to give material and financial aid themselves. The arguments will be similar to those used prior to 1963: that without them they will be prevented from undertaking effective casework. Nevertheless, Jordan's views are clearly attractive to others and they offer one solution to the dilemmas posed for social workers by financial aid.

Conclusions

Very little social work writing has concentrated firmly on financial aid. The subject usually has been treated indirectly or as a side issue. This has meant that social workers have received only very general guidance on the way they ought to use their powers.

Social work practice and financial aid

If social workers follow Jordan's lead and abandon the use of financial aid altogether then the absence of a firm body of theory covering such matters will be little missed. However, if this is not the case and social workers continue to use financial aid then there will be a need for better guidance. There will be a need for guidance on how financial aid activity can be used to further specifically social work objectives and how it can be used imaginatively integrated with other forms of social work activity.

Chapter six

Variations in the provision of financial aid

Although Section 1 of the Children and Young Persons Act 1963 and Sections 12 and 24 of the Social Work (Scotland) Act 1968 gave social service and social work departments the power to offer financial aid directly to clients they did not specify in any detail the occasions when a department must do so. The legislation enabled, but except in a very general sense, did not require local authorities to offer financial aid; considerable discretion was left in the hands of individual authorities. One of the results is that there have been major variations in the extent to which aid has been given by authorities.

The variations can be noted from the earliest years. For example, in 1965-6 three authorities gave more than £3,000 each (Lancashire, Coventry and Tower Hamlets) whereas four authorities spent less than £10 each (Cambridgeshire and Isle of Ely, Barrow-in-Furness, Canterbury and Hartlepool). By 1968-9 on average the totals were greater but the variations no less marked: thus, twelve authorities spent more than £5,000 each (Buckinghamshire, Kent, Lancashire, Somerset, Coventry, Barnet, Camden, Haringey, Lewisham, Southwark, Tower Hamlets and Wandsworth) while fourteen spent less than £100 each (Rutland, East Riding of Yorkshire, Barrow-in-Furness, Bury, Canterbury, Eastbourne, Great Yarmouth, Hartlepool, Huddersfield, Hull, Lincoln, Oldham, Sunderland and Wakefield). When these totals are standardized to take account of the population under 18 then the rank ordering alters but the variations are just as dramatic.

The most recent figures shows similar variations. Table 12 shows the highest and lowest spending authorities (per head of the population under 18) in England in 1974-5 and 1975-6. It is worth noting that the top ten spending authorities all spent more than £450 and £650 per 1,000 head of the population under 18 in 1974-5 and

Variations in the provision of financial aid

Table 12 Expenditure on financial aid through social work in
England under Section 1 of 1963 Children and Young Persons
Act: highest and lowest spending authorities 1974-5, 1975-6

	1974-5	1975-6
	Highest spending authorities in England*	
1	Hackney	Hackney
2	Hammersmith	Hammersmith
3	Camden	Dorset
4	Wandsworth	Camden
5	Westminster	Westminster
6	Harrow	Wandsworth
7	Kent	Hampshire
8	Hampshire	Kent
9	Dorset	Tower Hamlets
10	Oxfordshire	Avon†
(1 = Highest)		
	Lowest spending authorities in England*	
1	City of London	City of London
2	St Helens	St Helens
3	Durham	Knowsley
4	Isle of Wight	Isle of Wight
5	Solihull	Solihull
6	Kirklees	Northumberland
7	Tameside	Durham
8	Wigan	Bolton
9	Knowsley	Salford
10	Rotherham	Wigan
(1 = Lowest)		

*Based on those authorities for which figures were available for 1975 and
1976: expenditure per head of population under 18
†Includes amount spent on bed and breakfast accommodation
Source: Department of Health and Social Security, Children in Care of
Local Authorities, 1974-5, 1975-6

1975-6 respectively whereas the bottom ten authorities all spent less
than £12 and £16 per 1,000 head of the population under 18 in the
same periods.

Table 13 shows the position in Scotland in 1971 to 1973 inclusive:
the top ten and bottom ten spending authorities are listed. Again
massive variations in provision might be noted. Thus, whereas
Clydebank gave £24 per 100 head of population (Coatbridge £19 and
Sutherland £14), nine authorities (Ayr, Rutherglen, Argyll, Berwick,

Table 13   Expenditure on financial aid through social work in
Scotland under the provisions of Section 12 of the Social Work
(Scotland) Act 1968, in 1971, 1972 and 1973

	Average expenditure per 100 head of population 1971-3
Highest spending authorities	£
Clydebank	24
Coatbridge	19
Sutherland	14
Dumfries (borough)	11
Edinburgh	9
Glasgow	9
Dumbarton	7
Motherwell	7
Aberdeen (borough)	5
Aberdeen (county)	5
Lowest spending authorities	
Zetland	1
Ayr	0*
Rutherglen	0*
Argyll	0*
Berwick	0*
Caithness	0*
Dumfries (county)	0*
Perth	0*
Ross and Cromarty	0*
Wigtown	0*

*signifies less than £1
Source: Social Work Services Group, Scottish Social Work Statistics

Caithness, Dumfries, Perth, Ross and Cromarty and Wigtown) gave
less than £1. Using statistical measures, the distribution was highly
skewed (1971 2·985, 1972 2·989, 1973 3·877).

However, the extent of variations in expenditure is merely one
feature that needs to be noted: another is the relative consistency.
This can be seen in two ways. First, the number of times authorities
appear in either the top or bottom spenders lists might be referred
to. Thus it might be noted that Lancashire, Coventry and Tower
Hamlets appeared in the top spenders lists in both 1965-6 and
1968-9, while Barrow-in-Furness, Canterbury and Hartlepool
appeared in the bottom spenders lists in both years. The position in

Variations in the provision of financial aid

1974-5 and 1975-6 in England is not comparable with these earlier periods because of the changes that took place in local government structure, but if one simply looks at these two years it is worth recording that eight of the authorities that appeared in the top spenders list in 1974-5 did so again in 1975-6 and seven of the authorities that appeared in the bottom spenders list in 1974-5 did so again in 1975-6. The position is very similar in Scotland. A number of authorities, like Clydebank and Coatbridge were consistently high spenders while a number of others, like Ayr, Perth and Dumfries (county) were consistently low spenders. A second way of showing the consistency in variations is to refer to a mathematical measure which takes the spending of all authorities into account. The Spearman's rank correlation coefficient for expenditure in England in the years 1974-5 and 1975-6 is 0·9071 (significant at the 0·001 level) while the coefficient for expenditure in Scotland in the years 1971 and 1972 is 0·9235, in 1971 and 1973 is 0·8095, and in 1972 and 1973 is 0·8763 (all significant at the 0·001 level).

In the past there has been considerable interest amongst social scientists in variations in the provision of social services.[1] A number of items have been suggested that might help to explain the variations observed. Although all are not directly relevant to the provision of financial aid through social work, clearly some are: these will be reviewed below. For convenience the items have been grouped into four broad areas, though undoubtedly there are overlaps.

1 *The concentration of problems relevant to the provisions of financial aid*

One of the main justifications for the use of local authority rather than central government machinery, and for the granting of discretionary powers to local authorities, is the belief that this will enable the extent of the provision of services to be varied between areas to take account of different problems that might exist. It is felt that it is easier for a local authority to identify special problems and needs: it is also felt that they are more likely to be more open and responsive to demands for extra measures to deal with such problems. Clearly one is not talking here about merely any problems but about problems related to the services concerned.

Financial aid provided under the 1963 and the 1968 Acts is designed to enable authorities to deal better with welfare problems. In theory at least it is not an income maintenance provision: it is a provision to enable ancillary financial aid to be given. One might expect therefore that more aid would be needed, and more aid provided, in areas where there were a large number of 'social

80

problems' than in areas where there were a relatively small number. In England and Wales the 'problems' would be related to one particular client group, children, whereas in Scotland the problems could be related to any member of the community.

In practice, of course, financial aid may be used as an income maintenance service: the evidence to support this contention has already been reviewed. If this is the case then one might expect some relationship between the level of incomes in an authority (or at least the proportion of families with low incomes) and the provision of financial aid. Further, in practice there will often be an overlap between welfare and financial problems: the studies of multiple deprivation[2] have looked at this question in some detail. The two types of problems are often associated and may affect each other. Thus, even if financial aid is merely a welfare orientated and not an income maintenance service, it is likely that there will be some association between financial aid and the level of incomes in a community.

It has also been noted earlier that a great deal of financial aid is given to deal with rent and fuel debts. In many areas about 75 per cent of all aid is given to deal with such problems. The variations in the provision of financial aid, therefore, may be related to the prevalence of these problems in different areas. For example, it might be imagined that areas with high rents or those in which substantial rent increases have recently been experienced will provide a great deal of financial aid.

2 *Alternative provision*

Many other people who have looked at variations in the provision of social services between local authority areas have examined the possibility that such variations might be associated with the alternatives available.[3] Two contradictory lines of reasoning might be considered. The first is that financial aid might be a substitute for other provision. For example, it might be a substitute for institutional care and provision. One of the original aims of the 1963 legislation was to enable local authorities to prevent children being taken into care so as to reduce total expenditure in the long term. Maybe authorities that have little residential accommodation for children will need to make greater efforts to keep children out of care than those that have an abundance and therefore maybe they will spend more on financial aid through social work. If this is the case then one might expect a negative correlation between the provision of residential accommodation for children and the provision of financial aid through social work. Financial aid, of course, might be a substitute not only for other local authority provision but also for provision by voluntary and other statutory agencies. The need for co-ordination between local authorities and voluntary agencies was highlighted by the Home Office circular on the 1963 Act.[4] Thus one might argue that the correlation between financial aid and other provision should not be restricted to local authorities but should be extended to cover all alternative provision.

The second line of reasoning would follow a different kind of approach. This would suggest not that one kind of service is a substitute for another but rather that social services should be looked at as a whole. Relatively 'good' provision of financial aid through social work might be accompanied not by a 'weak' provision of possible substitutes but a similarly 'good' provision. The reason for this might be that the provision of both financial aid through social work and its substitutes are affected by the same variable: the welfare orientation of the authority. Thus, authorities might be classified as 'welfare' or 'non welfare orientated' with the result that relatively 'generous' provision of one type of service might be a good guide to those authorities that are relatively generous in the provision of all types of service.

3 *Political complexion of the authority*

The major political parties in Britain not only adopt different policies on specific issues but are also associated with different overall approaches to welfare. Broadly, the Conservative party, traditionally, has been associated with a 'residual', whereas the Labour party has been associated with an 'institutional' model of welfare.[5] If one followed this line then one might expect that one would be able to identify the 'welfare orientation' of the authority (as described in the last paragraph) by reference to its political complexion.

However, there are a number of qualifications that might have to be made to this rule. First, although an association between a particular model of welfare and a particular political party may be reasonable at the national level it might not be so compelling at the local level. There is often a divergence between national and local political attitudes and divergences on social questions are notorious. Although the divergences may be greatest on 'moral' social questions they are also often considerable on purely welfare matters. For instance, the belief in the need 'to stand on one's own feet' is often just as prevalent amongst 'self made' Labour as amongst 'self made' Conservative councillors.

Second, it is important to recognize that at the local, possibly even more than at the national level, policy can be influenced as much by personality as by doctrine. The 'local city boss' is often thought to be an American phenomenon but there are a number of British local authorities where a near equivalent can be found. Similarly local politics can be just as volatile as national politics. Relatively few authorities have been consistently controlled by one of the major political parties. The orientation to welfare of the authority, therefore, may be a reflection not only of the current but also of the previous dominant party.

Third, one needs to recognize that in some parts of Britain it is difficult to attach political labels. In many rural areas candidates offer themselves for election as 'independents': frequently though by no means always this is a pseudonym for Conservative. The picture has become even more complicated recently in Scotland and Wales with the emergence of nationalist parties. Both the main nationalist parties contain 'right' and 'left' wing subgroups.

4 Social work personnel

In most cases financial aid is only given under the 1963 and 1968 Acts by social work personnel. There are exceptions: the example of the financial aid group in Glasgow where clerical staff dealt with financial aid is covered more fully elsewhere. However, this was one of the few exceptions and has recently been modified itself. It might be imagined, therefore, that there could be a positive correlation between the number of social workers employed and the amount of aid given. Quite simply, more social workers might see more clients and therefore might in total give more financial aid.

However, there are other possibilities. Some commentators have suggested that financial aid is given by social workers as a way of dealing with a client when they are under pressure themselves because of a high caseload. Thus a social worker might give a client a small amount of financial aid simply to get the client 'off the books' or 'out of his hair'. If this were true, then the amount of financial aid given by an authority might be negatively correlated with the number of social workers employed.

Further, it is possible that certain types of social worker might react in such a fashion to pressure placed upon them more than others. For example, it might be suggested that unqualified social workers might give financial aid to relieve pressure more than qualified social workers because of their inexperience or their inability to deal with the situation in other ways. It might also be suggested that unqualified social workers are likely to be less certain of their position than qualified workers and as a result might be less willing to turn down a request from a client for financial aid for fear that their decision might be challenged at a later date. These arguments might also apply in a similar fashion to newly appointed social workers: on occasions the two types will coincide, but by no means always. It might be suggested that experience rather than qualification is frequently the crucial determinant of confidence.

Many of the items mentioned are difficult to quantify exactly. National or comprehensive figures are not always available. However, in other cases the position is not so difficult and at least useful indicators can be found. For instance, a number of measures of social and economic conditions are available and have been used in many other projects with reasonable effect.[6] As a result it is possible to attempt an evaluation of the extent to which some of the items mentioned appear to influence the payment of financial aid through social work.

Williams has attempted such an evaluation for the London boroughs.[7] She tried to relate the payment of financial aid to the social need of the area. Table 14 illustrates her results. From this table it can be seen that there is some relationship between financial aid and social need, though there is by no means a perfect correlation (in statistical terms the correlation coefficient was 0·66).

Other studies that have centred on social need have shown very similar results.[8] Social need explains some, but not all of the variation. For instance, while it is possible to explain the high spending of some of the London boroughs on the basis of social need, it is difficult to account for the low spending of Rotherham, Bolton, Wigan and St Helens in the same way.

If one looks beyond social need, at other variables, then the picture becomes even more difficult to disentangle. Labour dominated local authorities are represented amongst both the high and low spenders (the Inner London boroughs are high spenders and Labour dominated while boroughs like Rotherham, Wigan and Durham are low spenders and Labour dominated) as are Conservative dominated authorities (Westminster, Harrow and Kent are high spenders but Conservative dominated while the City of London, the Isle of Wight and Tameside are low spenders and have substantial Conservative representation). Similar comments can be made about levels of staffing and alternative provision.

It is somewhat easier to obtain comprehensive figures for the variables mentioned in Scotland than it is in England. As a result we attempted a major statistical examination of the correlation between the provision of financial aid through social work in Scotland and most of the variables previously mentioned. Table 15 shows the variables which offered the highest correlations with the provision of financial aid. From this table it can be seen that the most important variables were those which reflected social service provision, socio-economic conditions and the political complexion of the authority.

So far, all the attempts to correlate variables with the provision of

Table 14 Financial aid through social work and social need in the London boroughs, 1971-2

Borough	Expenditure per 1,000 pop. under 18 £	Rank for expenditure	Social needs* index rank
Hackney	251·78	8	1
Islington	248·76	9	2
Tower Hamlets	506·35	3	3
Newham	52·76	19	4
Lambeth	317·56	5	5
Haringey	109·25	15	6
Hammersmith	264·76	7	7
Brent	94·10	17	8
Wandsworth	241·66	10	9
Southwark	191·79	12	10
Westminster	629·38	2	11
Lewisham	137·17	13	12
Kensington	229·95	11	13
Greenwich	101·10	16	14
Ealing	498·62	4	15
Camden	820·23	1	16
Hounslow	26·77	26	17
Waltham Forest	32·01	24	18
Barking	42·41	20	19
Merton	41·90	21	20
Barnet	281·10	6	21
Richmond	6·53	30	22
Croydon	40·81	22	23
Harrow	15·17	29	24
Hillingdon	5·32	31	25
Enfield	68·50	18	26
Sutton	0	32	27
Redbridge	15·64	28	28
Bexley	17·74	27	29
Bromley	32·88	23	30
Kingston	130·41	14	31
Havering	28·73	25	32

*The index consisted of: men in unskilled/semi skilled jobs; households in overcrowded dwellings; households in dwellings lacking basic amenities; children in large families; population born in the New Commonwealth; children recently moved into the borough from elsewhere. Each variable was given an equal weighting
Source: F. Williams, 'Cash Assistance for Families', unpublished, quoted by R. Lister and T. Emmett, *Under the Safety Net*, Child Poverty Action Group, London, 1976

Variations in the provision of financial aid

Table 15   Financial aid through social work in Scotland correlated with a number of different variables

Measures	Correlation coefficient	Level of significance
Net social work expenditure	0·56048	0·00001
Revenue social work expenditure	0·51725	0·00004
Socio Economic Grouping 11	0·41214	0·00120
Percentage of Labour held seats*	0·43808	0·01613
Female employment rate	0·38868	0·00220
Female economic activity rates	0·37862	0·00282
Percentage dwellings owner occupied	0·36543	0·00386
Percentage dwellings over 1·5 persons per room	0·35490	0·00492

*Only calculated where political affiliations declared

financial aid through social work have been on a one to one basis. It is clear, though, that many of the variables overlap and are correlated with each other (the social need indicators are highly correlated with the political complexion of the authority). It is also clear that the variables might be associated with the provision of financial aid through social work in combination as well as singularly and in an indirect as well as a direct fashion.

A number of statistical techniques exist to enable one to deal with these complexities: they include factor analysis, multiple regression and path analysis. Some techniques complement but some are alternatives to others. We have tried a number of different strategies to explain the variations in the provision of financial aid in Scotland. This is not the place to examine them in any detail[9] but we might record our broad conclusions. In general we found it possible to explain a fairly high proportion of the variance noted by looking at the effect of a number of factors (broadly at measures of need and methods of provision) in combination and directly and indirectly. We would suggest that the most important group of factors can be gathered under the vague heading of 'need' (in particular economic need).

However, while broadly we can confirm that need, in particular economic need, is a major influence on the variation in provision, we cannot argue that we can offer a complete explanation on this basis: something else seems to be affecting the picture. Briefly what we would suggest is that in many areas social service and social work departments provide financial aid in reaction to demands made upon them as a result of the 'need' (especially the 'economic need') in their area. These demands might be made by clients on their own initiative or by clients reacting to suggestions or directions from other agencies like the Supplementary Benefits Commission, the housing department or the fuel authority. In some authorities, though, this does not seem to happen. To understand why it happens in some authorities but not in others one needs to refer to the way decisions are made in social work departments. In particular one needs to look at the different parties that influence decisions, inside and outside the organization, and at the level at which decisions are made.

Chapter seven

Decision making

Introduction

Many writers have examined decision making in the social services. Some have tried to apply models developed from the business enterprise, others have recognized the major distinctive features of social service organizations.[1] A number of writers have pointed to the way that employees in the social services are able to alter the intentions of policy makers.[2]

Our discussion of decision making in financial aid will use the model proposed by Donnison *et al.*[3] as a starting point. This model was developed after an analysis of a series of case studies of innovation in social service departments. It highlights three main groups of participants; the controllers of resources (local councillors), the providers of service (social workers) and the determiners of demand (clients). The authors argued that effective policy frequently was made not by the controllers of resources but by the providers of service. There were a number of reasons for this. First, social policy is rarely precisely defined; in part this is because it is difficult to predict the needs to be met and social policy is often innovative, although on occasions it is also because policy has to be vague if it is to secure the agreement of the variety of different people and interest groups involved. This means that it is difficult for controllers of resources to lay down specific objectives for providers to follow and to check that they do so. Second, the controllers of resources permit the providers to have a degree of discretion because they recognize that they are professionals or semi-professionals with specialist knowledge of their own. Third, the providers frequently work in a decentralized administrative structure which militates against detailed control of their day to day activities. Fourth, the providers of the service claim to be in close contact with the determiners of demand and to need flexibility so that they can respond quickly to changing needs amongst the client group.

This three part model has many general attractions. As Donnison *et al.* claim, it enables one to identify the crucial role of the providers of the service. 'They are not simply the instruments of their governing body—an impersonal link between the committee and its clients. They create and continually modify the service.'[4] Other studies have shown how employees can frustrate the wishes of employers and how informal rules can develop. Such studies have not been confined to business organizations; Blau's classic study examined work in a public assistance agency.[5] However, Donnison's study goes one stage further by showing how local authority social services provide an environment especially conducive to growth in the power and scope of the providers.

Another general attraction of this model is that it enables one to escape from the familiar dichotomies: 'formal-informal', 'bureaucrats-public', and 'state-citizen'. Again, as Donnison *et al.* claim, such dichotomies establish pervasive, but erroneous, assumptions about the nature of the administrative process.

More specifically the model has many attractions for a study of financial aid through social work. There are many aspects of such a study which seem to fit neatly into the Donnison model. For example, the aims of financial aid through social work have rarely been spelt out: the 1963 and 1968 Acts did little more than express a general view that financial aid should be used to benefit the welfare of the client group concerned, while subsequent official memoranda have done little to clarify the position further. There is evidence that the framers of the Acts had only a very general view about what was intended. Discussing the 1968 Scottish Act, Carmichael, one of the architects of the Act, has confessed that they had little conception of the needs to be met by Section 12 when it was drafted.[6] It was a general enabling clause dealing with social welfare; it did not specify to whom or for what aid was to be given, nor, in any detail, in what circumstances. Similarly, the service is controlled formally by local authority councillors, laymen without specialist social work knowledge, and provided by social workers who at least frequently claim to be professionals or semi-professionals.

This should not be taken to imply, though, that there are no criticisms or modifications to be made to the Donnison *et al.* thesis either in general or as far as financial aid is concerned. In general, one might note that by no means all of the case studies Donnison *et al.* put forward fully support their model. Their study of developments in a children's department is probably the most convincing but even in this case the model seems to place too much emphasis on social workers as transmitters of clients' needs and too little on social workers' own views as determinants of policy.

More specifically, as far as financial aid is concerned, the model seems to place too much emphasis on the social service organization and too little on the environment in which it has to work. There are many important points of contact between the organization and its environment; one such point of contact, clients, was recognized by Donnison *et al.* However, there are others, and in the case of financial aid one further set appears to be particularly important; the relationship between the social service or social work department and what we might term 'other organizations in contact'. Centrally, we are referring to bodies like the Supplementary Benefits Commission, housing departments and fuel authorities. From earlier discussion it appears that these bodies have a crucial role to play in determining the needs to be met by social service and social work departments.

We shall adopt, then, a four part model to analyse decision making on financial aid. The four part model will involve the controllers of resources (local councillors), the providers of services (social workers), the determiners of demand (clients) and other agencies in contact (primarily the Supplementary Benefits Commission, the fuel and housing authorities). We are not suggesting that there are no overlaps between these groups, nor that other factors cannot influence decisions, simply that such an approach might provide a useful way of ordering the material involved.

The discussion itself will be based on material collected from a variety of sources. For example, we have conducted in depth studies and surveys in a number of social work departments, we have had numerous discussions with personnel in many others and consulted members of the main professional organizations. Where relevant we also refer to other research and other writing.

Necessarily we do not attempt to present a description of a typical department or try to assess in a statistical fashion the extent to which features we note are representative of general practice. Rather we have concentrated on highlighting important aspects of decision making, explaining why they exist and assessing what impact they have.

Controllers of resources

Responsibility for formal policy making on financial aid has been devolved from the national to the local government. In practice, from the examination we have made, it appears that the extent of formal policy at the local authority level is extremely rudimentary. At this level there appears to be what might be termed a 'policy vacuum'.

Most local authorities restrict policy making in this area to the setting down of cash limits for total expenditure on financial aid and individual limits for expenditure by different grades of social worker. However, even these limits may have restricted practical value. In one authority we looked at no formal budgetary allocation was made for financial aid: we were told that instead the finance department made a 'guestimate' of likely expenditure. In others, departments often exceeded their budgetary allocation: financial aid was recognized as an area that 'could not easily be controlled'. Such practices are beginning to be looked at more sceptically and it is possible that with local authority budgets generally becoming tighter, financial aid allocations will be monitored more rigorously in the future, though in our work we found only the seeds of such moves.

The efficacy of cash limits for individual social workers seems to vary considerably from authority to authority. In one of the authorities we studied social workers had no formal right to authorize aid on their own, but in practice this rule frequently was bypassed. Social workers often authorized aid, without consultation 'in an emergency' or when a senior member of staff 'was not available'. In some instances it is clear that social workers authorized aid on their own initiative when, strictly, they were not permitted to do so, because they were confident that their actions would be subsequently ratified by a senior colleague. Of course, such practice is by no means universal and depends on the relationship existing between different grades of staff. Again, in one authority we studied, all decisions on aid exceeding £75 had to be approved by the social work committee but in fact the committee did not discuss any financial aid cases during one nine month period we examined even though a number of grants or loans exceeding £75 had been made. Sometimes the need to refer such matters to the committee is bypassed by the chairman acting on behalf of the committee. In others even this does not happen: the chairman allows the director of social work to act on his behalf.

However, the important point is that whether or not such budgetary allocations or cash limits are effective, they can hardly be described as meaningful policy making. Budgetary allocations frequently are more a reflection of previous spending patterns than conscious decisions about competitive areas of interest: limits on the powers of individual social workers usually are merely a codification of practice suggested by senior social work personnel. In essence, local authority policy, where it exists, is simply negative: it merely states when money cannot and by whom it cannot be spent. There are few authorities which have laid down a positive policy arguing how financial aid might be used to increase social welfare.

In some instances an even more extreme picture might be painted. We undertook a survey of councillors of one local authority to ascertain their knowledge and views of financial aid through social work. We divided them into two groups: those who were or had been members of a social work committee and those who had not. As one might suspect those in the latter group had least knowledge of financial aid. A majority could not recall ever having discussed the issue on a council committee, with colleagues or with council officials. Only a minority knew that social workers had the power to give financial aid directly and of those who knew that social workers had such power few could give a detailed description of policy or powers: in fact, many gave an incorrect description. However, although those councillors who were or had been members of a social work committee had greater knowledge, in many cases it was still fairly rudimentary. Over a third of this group could not recall ever having discussed financial aid, either on a social work committee, or elsewhere, and a similar proportion were unaware that social workers had the ability to give financial aid directly. Their detailed knowledge of policy was poor: nobody was able to quote the same cash limits as we had been given by professional staff and a sizeable number quoted policy that was incorrect in terms of the groups who could or could not be helped.

There appear to be a number of reasons for this situation. One lies in the interest and aptitude of the councillors themselves. Again, we might refer to evidence gained from our survey. A majority of all councillors, and about a third of councillors who were or had been on a social work committee, expressed reservations about their ability to make judgments on social work matters. Many felt that their training and background was inadequate and decisions were best left to professionals. Handler has argued[7] that there might be a distinction on such matters between councillors representing different political parties. He suggests that Labour councillors might be less deferential to professional expertise than their Conservative counterparts. We do not feel that we have sufficient information either to confirm or to dispute this hypothesis. However, we found that many councillors of all political persuasions felt happier about making decisions on individual cases rather than broad policy issues: they would much rather have discussed whether individual A or individual B should be given aid than general policy. This assessment was confirmed by many of the senior social work officials we spoke to. We were told of a number of cases where councillors had acted as advocates for constituents on financial aid. Further, his description has links with the results of earlier research[8] which showed that most councillors were attracted to stand for election because of their interest in detailed local issues rather than broad policy matters.

It is also worth while making comment at this juncture on the reasons why councillors joined a social work committee. Here we were dealing with relatively small numbers, so our results need to be interpreted cautiously. However, we noted that few of the councillors we spoke to owed their membership of a social work committee to a specific interest in, or desire to take decisions about, social work. Frequently councillors found themselves on the social work committee because they had been allocated (on occasions it seemed almost randomly) to that area by the party caucus.

Nevertheless, while the interest and aptitude of councillors must be one of the major reasons why there is little in the way of formal local authority policy in this area, two other factors need to be taken into account. First, while financial aid through social work may be an important issue to social workers and may take up a great deal of their time, it seems relatively unimportant to many local authority councillors (even those interested in social work and broad policy questions). It takes up a very small proportion of the social work let alone the local authority budget (in most authorities it accounts for substantially less than 1 per cent of the former) and most councillors have been taught to measure importance by cost. The only exception to this rule is where a scandal arises or there is concerted pressure from constituents but even when this occurs it is likely to lead to intervention on individual cases rather than a discussion of general policy.

The second reason refers to social workers themselves. The reservations many councillors have about their ability to make policy on social work issues often are encouraged by social workers. The emphasis on professionalism and an exclusive body of knowledge only available to social workers has cemented this tendency but it has always been present, if only because many senior social work staff have felt that councillors are ill equipped to deal with social work and are doubtful of the usefulness of aspects of the service. In fact, in our survey of councillors we found little evidence to support this latter contention. Most councillors were quick to support the work of social work departments, although clearly some had reservations about particular aspects of policy, as was evidenced by the number who agreed with the statements that 'social workers are too soft with their clients' and 'social workers cause more problems than they solve'. However there is also evidence to support the suggestion that if councillors were encouraged to make policy on social work many would want to extend their influence to an extent unacceptable to many social workers. Although as we have mentioned many councillors had reservations about their ability to make decisions on social work, some did not: one councillor told us that he had wanted to sit on the social work committee because he had been a teacher and consequently knew far more about social work than 'some of those inexperienced social workers'. It is comments such as this that have led many senior social workers to try to prevent councillors 'interfering' in the area of social work. One senior social worker we spoke to told us that he had made deliberate attempts to reduce the freedom of councillors to discuss social work issues in committee. He argued that previously social work staff frequently had been forced to justify individual casework decisions, a situation which he found disruptive and unacceptable.

The providers of the services

The discussion to this point has suggested an absence of all but the most rudimentary formal local authority policy on financial aid through social work. It has also suggested that on occasions even such policy as exists may be circumvented. A further example reinforces this point. In one local authority the social work committee had decided that aid should be given only in the form of 'loans'. However, social workers effectively evaded this policy by giving a proportion of aid as 'non recoverable' loans.

Considerable scope exists, therefore, in most local authority departments for headquarters social work personnel to establish policy themselves; often they are in a position to lay down firm guidelines on major aspects of financial aid and in a number of cases this opportunity has been well taken. Headquarters staff may specify the types and groups of clients who may or may not be considered for aid, the procedure to be followed when a request for aid is received, other agencies that should be contacted when aid is requested (such as the Supplementary Benefits Commission, the housing department or the fuel authority) and they may amplify the rules governing cash limits for individual social workers originally established by the local authority social work committee. We have visited a number of departments in which such policy has had a major impact on practice.

However, it is probably fair to argue that we have seen more departments where headquarters policy generally has not been applied. There are many reasons for this. For example, we were told of a policy decision in one department to restrict financial aid to certain categories of client (the very young and the elderly) and then to restrict aid to extreme cases (aid was only to be given for fuel debts if there were young children in a house where electricity was the only source of heating and cooking). In practice, this policy decision proved to be too severe and gradually the number of exceptions increased, eventually to such an extent that the original policy was virtually abandoned.

In other authorities we have been told that policy decisions have been ignored because there has been no effective means of checking that they have been adhered to. In this context the importance of good record keeping and full documentation might be noted. If few or inadequate written records of cases dealt with and decisions made are kept then it may be impossible to monitor decision making and ensure that it is in line with official policy.

In still other authorities, policy decisions have been ignored because they have been felt to be impractical. For example, in one authority we looked at it was stated that all decisions on financial aid should be made after consultation with a senior member of staff. This placed serious restrictions on both basic grade social workers and senior personnel. The former had a duty to find a senior member of staff, even in an emergency, to discuss a case with him while the latter had a duty to make themselves available or ensure that they could be contacted at all times. In practice, neither side found these obligations easy to accept and the policy has been avoided.

Frequently formal lines of authority and decision making structures are avoided in social work departments by the development of informal networks. In many instances such networks are based on friendship patterns or functional alliances, but in certain circumstances they may follow old organizational lines. Most social service and social work departments have experienced two major organizational upheavals in the recent past, the unification of local authority social service functions and the restructuring consequent upon the reorganization of local government. In a number of cases we noted informal networks based on old organizational structures. Thus, a social worker might 'jump' stages in the official decision making hierarchy by consulting directly with a colleague who was 'his senior' in an old department.

We also noted in many authorities that policy decisions of headquarters social work staff were poorly understood by fieldwork staff. In a survey of social workers we found a number of respondents who claimed to be unaware that policy decisions had ever been made and far more who were unclear as to the nature of that policy. In some authorities policy is written down and enshrined in official documents. However, frequently such documents are not easily available: in our survey of social workers we found few respondents who had seen such documents: most had heard about policy by word of mouth.

In such circumstances, team leaders, area officers and the like may assume a role of major importance. They are the main channel of communication for decisions between headquarters personnel and field staff. In certain circumstances they may be able to reinterpret official policy: at the very least they can put their own gloss on it or adapt it to meet their own particular needs. In one authority we were able to note this happening ourselves. The policy of the authority had been decided by headquarters social work personnel and was meant to apply throughout the region. In practice, the policy in one team was radically different from another, each being decided by the team leader.

Of course, it would be unwise to characterize the senior area or team staff simply as intermediaries in the communication system who usurp additional power. In some authorities effective policy making is formally delegated to them. They are recognized to be members of staff with experience in many fields who are in an excellent position to note developments and needs at the local level. Thus, it was not merely that they 'informally' adapted headquarters policy on the type of client who should be given financial aid: it was more that they were often expected to make such decisions.

Their effective power, though, like that of headquarters staff, may not be as great as the official organizational structure might suggest. For example, while they may find it relatively easy to ensure that certain types of client are not awarded aid against their wishes, they might find it far more difficult to ensure that aid is given to a particular group of clients they favour. Their powers, to a large extent, are negative. If a social worker decides on his own initiative to refuse a request for aid, then the senior social worker may never hear of the instance. Few departments have procedures where all requests for aid have to be looked at by a senior member of staff, and even where such rules exist, it is relatively easy for them to be avoided if the social worker persuades the client that there is no point in making a 'formal application'.

Senior staff may also find it difficult to supervise decisions which are made at some distance from the central office or which are made 'in an emergency'. Of course, the term 'emergency' is imprecise; in practice a great deal more of social work activity can be classified as 'emergency' than might at first be thought. Initially one might merely think of the periods out of normal office hours when social workers are on 'stand by' and expected to deal with problems on their merits. Similarly one might visualize the kind of problems faced in departments where because of their geographical position they have to deal with a large number of people temporarily visiting the area (and turning up without any planned accommodation) or in transit through it. However, especially in the case of financial aid, a large proportion of social work involves reacting to immediate pressures rather than planning 'promotional' activity, and such immediate pressures cannot be left while the wheels of the formal organizational machinery slowly grind in their normal way.

In practice senior staff may influence decision making on financial aid more through the general ethos they can create than by formal rules or checks. For example, if senior staff are unhappy about the amount of financial aid being given this may not be expressed in any official document but simply may be reflected in a degree of tardiness about approving requests for financial aid or in informal discussion. In one authority such a view was encouraged by the length of time it took to get approval for financial aid. If a social worker pressed a case or waited long enough then it was unlikely that his request would be refused. Nevertheless, the fact that it took so long for requests to be approved created an atmosphere that had an impact on decision making. One field social worker commented that 'it was easier to get a ticket to the moon' than approval to give financial aid. Further, in another authority we tried to discover what happened when a request for approval for financial aid was turned down by a senior member of staff. The reply was that this never happened because requests would only be made when it was known that they would be accepted.

It is also important to recognize that decisions on financial aid need not be made only either by senior staff or in accordance with official policy on the one hand, or by basic grade staff informally evading official policy on the other. On occasions decisions might be made after a period of negotiation between basic grade and senior staff. Such negotiations may take the form of a basic grade social worker acting as an advocate for the client with the senior social worker. He may even adopt a bargaining stance, initially asking for more than he expects to get or will settle for. Both the senior and basic grade social worker may have a stake in eventually reaching a compromise agreement. They have to maintain a continuing working relationship and each relies on the other for information and guidance. Further, the negotiation between the basic grade and senior social worker need not be the end of the road. Negotiations may have to continue afterwards at a higher level and at this stage the senior social worker may have to put forward the views of his more junior colleague.

Finally we need to consider the situation which exists in many authorities where neither headquarters nor senior staff attempt to determine policy. The initiative is left to the more junior fieldwork staff. There are a number of possible reasons for this. For example, senior staff may not feel competent to determine policy in such an area. It has been suggested that this has been a particular problem in Scotland where ex-probation officers have taken senior positions (probation officers were taken into the new unified social work departments in Scotland, but not in England) for they had little experience of financial aid in their previous posts. Alternatively, senior and headquarters staff may simply feel that financial aid is not important enough to command their attention or that basic grade staff are in a better position to assess demand and determine policy. Whatever the reason, it is clear that in many authorities little or no policy is determined by senior or headquarters staff and basic grade social workers are left to make decisions without any control or guidance. In such circumstances what attitudes and pressures determine the decisions of basic grade staff?

Most studies of professional staff stress the importance of the professional norms and culture in determining policy. The professional community is felt to have views about developments over a wide area and these views frequently pervade the organization in which an individual may work. The individual worker is seen as the Trojan horse bringing in the views of his colleagues from outside the organization.

Earlier, we reviewed what major social work texts had to say on financial aid. We argued that relatively few post Second World War texts spent a great deal of time on the topic. Some general guidance was offered but this was limited and far from comprehensive. More recently a number of writers have argued that financial aid should be separated from social work or only used with great caution; such arguments seem to find considerable support. Similarly, recently an attempt has been made to establish a cash code for social workers by the British Association of Social Workers.[9] However, it would be difficult to argue that there is a clear or detailed view in the literature which might help social workers to make decisions on financial aid.

Similarly, little is imparted on financial aid in the professional training of social workers. We have looked at a number of professional courses, surveyed their products and discussed past training with current social workers. We have no doubt that general views on social work affect attitudes towards financial aid, but in almost all cases, we were told that the question of financial aid had never been discussed directly. The most that might have been experienced was a general discussion in which views relevant to financial aid might have been expressed. Often, though, the people we surveyed said that they were taught or discussed nothing of relevance for financial aid. This leads to a wide diversity of views on financial aid amongst the products of professional social work courses. When we asked whether aid should be given in certain circumstances or not and why, frequently we met a 'don't know' or 'unsure' reply: when a more definite reply was given the spread of answers was bewildering and showed little in the way of an easily understandable pattern.

Social workers' attitudes may be influenced by the views expressed by colleagues within as well as those expressed by colleagues outside the organization. In one or two instances we have noted that fairly formal consultative structures have been devised by offices to deal with financial aid. In one team decisions on financial aid were only made after a 'team meeting': in another decisions would only be made after consultation with at least one other member of staff. Such formal consultative arrangements can provide useful supportive structures especially for social workers unsure about their role. Even when they do not exist, informal discussion may take place on financial aid between colleagues in one office. However, such discussion is by no means universal and depends partly on the stability of staff. Low staff turnover enables friendship patterns to develop and encourages informal discussion of problem areas of work. In many departments, though, staff turnover is high and prevents such developments.

One of the more important influences on social workers' attitudes towards financial aid appears to be their own background and their own views on society and human behaviour. Many of the discussions we had with social workers brought out views based on the likelihood of clients reacting to a 'firm lead', the willingness of clients to help themselves, the 'worthiness' of particular causes or groups. Some of these views may be linked to different professional experiences; ex-probation officers might have a different set of views from ex-child care officers. Yet, in most instances, such professional histories seemed to be obscured and overlaid by fairly individualistic criteria.

However, it would be a mistake if the impression were left that social workers have firm views on financial aid, whatever the source of such views. Our researches showed that most social workers were unsure and anxious about financial aid. Many claimed to be unsure as to what criteria should be used when making decisions. Some were particularly unhappy about making decisions in a face to face situation and tried to avoid reaching any conclusion at that point in time. In such instances decisions are delayed; a senior officer may be blamed as the cause of the trouble. Others felt the pressures to such an extent that they gave aid because 'they were afraid not to'; it is often far easier to give something, even if only a little, than it is to refuse a request altogether. The anxieties felt by social workers are reflected in their answers to our questions about who should be responsible for making decisions on financial aid. The vast majority of basic grade social workers requested more guidance from senior personnel and the majority wanted decision making taken out of their own hands. Few seemed willing to complain if their scope for manoeuvre were severely restricted. Thus, although we have previously noted that social workers can avoid official policy, the picture we are painting, for some areas, is not one of basic grade social workers devising mechanisms to subvert official policy, rather it is one where frequently basic grade social workers are left to make decisions with what they feel to be inadequate guidance. In such circumstances they are particularly open to pressures from clients and outside agencies.

It might reasonably be argued that the anxieties and pressures we have described are more likely to be felt by young social workers and recent recruits. To a large extent this is so, but in our research we noted that many older and established social workers were far from happy about the extent to which they were expected to make decisions on financial aid. A number of them, despite their general experience had not been called on to use financial aid in the past and as a result it was almost as novel to them as to their more junior colleagues. It is also worth while noting that the bulk of clients who request financial aid are seen by fairly junior and inexperienced staff. Long service and merit in social work departments are frequently rewarded by promotion to administrative work.

Determiners of service

The public in general appear to have a very sketchy and often erroneous conception of social work and the social services. Frequently the term 'the welfare' is used to refer to social services in general and knowledge of the distinction between social work and social security is poor. Certainly there is little evidence that the bulk of the population have any knowledge of the detailed provisions permitting social workers to give financial aid. A number of surveys[10] have shown that there is considerable confusion amongst the general public between social service departments and the Supplementary Benefits Commission, and it has been suggested that reorganization might have exacerbated the problem.

In our research we found little eagerness amongst social workers to change this position. While some might have been keen to improve general awareness of the structure and functions of the social services, few wanted to publicize the details of the power of social workers to give financial aid. At one level this might seem curious given the commitment of many social workers and some social work departments to welfare rights. Many senior social workers and directors of social work were not only unenthusiastic about such publicity but were actually hostile to the idea. They suggested that extra publicity would merely increase the number of clients for a service about which they were dubious anyway.

However, a distinction needs to be made between the public in general and the public in contact. While the public in general may have little detailed knowledge of the organization and operation of the social services, often the position is very different as far as the public in contact are concerned. Evidence suggests that in many cases there is a fairly high level of awareness and in some cases detailed knowledge is held. For example, we have already noted that in one local authority a system was introduced so that financial aid cases were examined only on one particular day, and then by a team meeting. A number of instances were reported of clients approaching social workers for financial aid and stressing that their claim must be processed in time to be determined on the day of the meeting. Further, in our survey of financial aid cases in one Scottish local authority (reported in chapter 3) we noted that there were a very high proportion of self referrals, and although we questioned whether the figures quoted were a true reflection of the position there is little doubt that many clients were aware of the provision enabling social workers to grant financial aid.

The absence of a firm body of rules or guidelines governing financial aid in many social work departments means that the way a claim or approach is proceeded with will depend, to a large extent, on the relationship between the social worker and the client. We have already noted some of the factors that influence the attitude and behaviour of the social worker. We have also stressed the amount of variation between social workers. There is a similar amount of variation between clients. Some clients are excellent advocates: they may have learnt their technique through years of contact with public agencies of one kind or another. Most social workers are able to recount tales of particular clients who are able to present the details of a case in such a way that even the most sceptical observer would find it hard not to feel sympathetic. Some clients are aware of the need to approach different social workers in different ways and highlight particular features of their case. For example, in the case of a financial aid application they may be aware of the value of stressing the danger to young children if help is not given. However, other clients are extremely poor advocates. Their knowledge of the social work department and the way it works is poor: they are unaware of the key words and phrases which can mean the difference between success and failure for a financial aid application. Numerous studies have shown that there is no relationship between the need for a social service and the ability to obtain it.[11] Frequently the people who need a service most receive the poorest response because they lack the skills necessary to determine what is available and how it might be obtained.

One of the major criticisms levelled at financial aid through social work is that the client has no recourse if he is dissatisfied with the treatment he receives. We know of no social work department which publishes details of the criteria by which it gives financial aid (even where such criteria exist) and none where a formal appeals system operates. We found that few basic grade social workers objected to the idea of an appeals system but many senior staff adopted a different view. One director of a social work department told us that an appeals system would be illogical and unworkable; how can you appeal when there are no criteria against which the original decision can be judged?

Clients may also be vulnerable to the social worker who wants to redefine his position. We came across a number of social workers who appeared to believe that financial aid problems inevitably were merely a cover for a more deep-seated personal problem. Of course, in some cases such a diagnosis may have been correct: in others it was probably a far from accurate assessment. Sometimes the attitude of the social worker has more to do with the kind of training received than the problem presented by the client.[12] One need not imply Machiavellian motives to question whether it is right to assume deeper personal problems on all occasions. However, again, clients vary in their ability to handle such a reaction. Undoubtedly some would simply leave the department outraged, threatening to take the matter to their local councillor or MP. At the other extreme, some would simply be confused or bow to what appeared to be superior knowledge. They might also cherish the hope that some time in the future, if they accept casework, then financial aid might be forthcoming.

Possibly more frequent is the occasion when a client's problem is not redefined but simply extended. The social worker need not say that financial help is not needed but rather that if the need for further help in the future is to be avoided then other action has to be taken as well. Handler has described the way in which social workers can coerce a client into accepting such additional guidance.[13]

However, the term coercion probably overstates what happens in many cases. Social workers frequently do not explicitly or implicitly threaten a client to persuade him to accept financial aid: rather financial aid is simply used as a way of making contact or gaining entry. For example, a social worker may give a client a loan and arrange to visit the client regularly to collect repayments. Such visits may enable the social worker to meet the client regularly and may enable him to discuss other issues or elicit information on other problems.

Once again clients vary in their reaction to such situations. Some may be willing and able to inform the social worker that no further help or advice is required. However, it will take a fairly confident and strong willed client to adopt such a stance. He has been placed in the position of debtor to the authority and whether or not this makes him vulnerable in a formal sense he may well feel or be made to feel that he should accept guidance.

We are not in a position to say with certainty how frequently the situations discussed above arise. However, we can point to three factors which militate against them arising as frequently as some might imagine. First, if a social worker is to redefine or extend a client's problem then he must have a clear idea himself of his aims and the theory on which he is basing his action. In the previous section we noted that some social workers have a clear view about how to approach financial aid, but that possibly more do not. They feel inadequate and unsure and have no clear philosophy to enforce on an unwilling client. Second, a great deal of financial aid, as we have already noted, is given as the result of pressure, often in an 'emergency' or 'semi-emergency' situation. In such circumstances the social worker often merely reacts to the circumstances facing him: he has no time to think of alternative strategies. Third, many social workers (though, of course, not all) have high caseloads. Redefining or extending a client's problem will mean adding to this caseload. Many social workers therefore will not have the time, even if they have the inclination, to adopt such a strategy. It is usually far easier and less time consuming to give a little financial help than to offer casework assistance.

While attention needs to be paid in detail to the social worker/ client relationship there are a number of other areas of interest. In particular, clients frequently are one of the major sources of information for the social worker about social conditions and problems in his area. Of course, social workers have many other sources of information: they may live in the local community themselves, they will probably meet a variety of people outside work on a social basis, they may read the local press and they may be presented with research reports. Nevertheless, clients are still one of the major sources of information available about local social conditions. In this instance, the important factor is not the behaviour or ability of a particular client but the aggregate number or percentages dealt with. If a social worker is constantly faced with clients demanding help with electricity bills then it is difficult to believe that he is not likely to be persuaded that fuel payments are a major problem in his area. Similarly, if a social worker is constantly faced with clients claiming that they cannot manage to live on Supplementary Benefits allowances it is difficult to believe that this is not likely to influence his view of the adequacy of such allowances.

Further, the sheer number of clients approaching a social worker for aid of any kind may have an effect on the decisions he makes. As we noted in the last section if he feels under pressure then a social worker might well be persuaded to give financial aid to clients to 'get them off his books' or as an alternative to other aid. If nothing else, he might feel unable to examine their cases in as much detail as normally would be expected.

Decision making

In some ways clients are merely acting as transmission agents in this area. One may argue that their own characteristics, relatively, have little impact. Of course, some clients may be able to deal better with higher electricity charges or all electric heating than others, but it is doubtful if individual differences can have more than a marginal effect on the nature of the overall problem as presented to the social worker. In this instance clients are largely reflecting the conditions existing in the local community and the policies of particular agencies in contact.

Other agencies in contact

The work of social service departments overlaps with and is influenced by that of many other agencies. In relation to financial aid, a number of agencies in contact influence decisions made in important respects. Their influence can be narrowed down to three main areas.

First, the other agencies may draw the attention of clients to the provisions that enable social service departments to give financial aid. Such instances are numerous. For example, one electricity board prints a statement on disconnection notices drawing the attention of clients to the help that might be available from social work departments. Many other agencies go further than this and firmly direct a client to the social service department. Sometimes this is because they claim that they cannot offer help whereas the social service department should be able to do so: this frequently occurs when social security officers claim that to offer aid for a particular contingency would be contrary to the Commission's regulations. On other occasions this may be because the social service department is the only agency to offer an emergency service. We have heard of a number of instances when the police have referred clients to the social work department because it was the only agency to offer an emergency service of the type required. On still other occasions it is because the agency or agent is recognized to be in a good position to identify clients who would not normally consider approaching the social service or social work department direct and thus is encouraged to refer clients to the department. Home helps, health visitors, nurses and doctors play important roles in this direction.

In Scotland, the social work department's ability to offer emergency aid may have a greater impact than in England. In Scotland, an agreement was reached between the directors of social work and a number of other public agencies that when a case arose which was 'marginal' in terms of which agency should take responsibility, the agency of 'first contact' would deal with the case. Clearly, if the social work department has a more efficient emergency service than other public utilities then it is more likely to be the agency of 'first contact' than would otherwise be the case.

Second, other agencies in contact may influence financial aid through social work by actions they take which cause 'problems' for clients. Note has been taken already that a great deal of financial aid is given to deal with rent and fuel arrears. To an extent these 'problems' may be the result of the action of other agencies. At one level, if a fuel authority raises its tariffs or a housing department raises its rents, this may result in more people being unable to meet rent and fuel bills and, as a consequence, approaching the social work department for help. Again, if a rent or a fuel authority changes its method of collecting monies this may affect the number of people who encounter problems with rent and fuel bills: more frequent collection may be a kind of enforced budgeting whereas less frequent collection places more reliance on a person's ability to allocate resources and save. Of course, it would be impossible to say that such actions and decisions 'cause problems': many other factors intervene and have an effect. Nevertheless, such actions and decisions, in certain circumstances, can have an important impact and can precipitate action.

Agencies in contact may also affect the task of social service departments by their reactions to the problems presented by their own clients. Again, the fuel and rent authorities provide the best examples. If a rent authority determines that it will evict in cases of serious rent arrears then it is likely that one result will be an increase in the number of clients who approach the social work department for financial aid. Other results may include a reduction in the number of clients accumulating rent arrears. However, it is difficult to believe that the threat of punishment alone will lead to an elimination of rent arrears. Similar comments can be made about the policy of fuel authorities on arrears and disconnections.

It would be a mistake though to look at the relationship between social service departments and public utilities in this area simply in terms of the way the latter influence the former. Of course the policy of public utilities towards problems presented by their own clients will affect the social work department: however, the policy adopted by the social work department towards clients presenting problems of fuel and rent arrears may also affect the attitude of the public utilities. Earlier we noted that if the public utility knows that the social work department will deal with clients with rent or fuel arrears, then it is far easier for it to take a firm line. On the other hand, evidence has been presented from a number of social work departments that when they have said that as a matter of policy they will not help clients with fuel or rent arrears, the public utility has felt it necessary to change its stand. In essence the public utilities recognize that in many cases help has to be given: as publicly responsible bodies they cannot ignore this fact. The stand they take is not designed to ensure that a client does not receive help: it is designed to ensure that they do not have to take the responsibility for giving such help.

Third, agencies in contact may affect decisions made by social service departments on financial aid by the extent to which they provide alternative sources of assistance. Again, the best known alternative source of assistance in most financial aid cases has been identified, the Supplementary Benefits Commission. Frequently its policy on assistance is a crucial factor in determining whether a client will approach the social work department for financial aid.

However, other agencies are also important. Many voluntary societies have sources of income which can be used to assist clients. Most social workers are aware of the sources that exist in their area and will examine the possibility of obtaining such help before recommending that aid be given by the local authority. Important charities include ex-servicemen's and religious organizations. Many charities provide aid in kind rather than cash; for example, some will provide shelter or meals. Although aid in kind is not always a substitute for cash, often it can be: this is true whether the aid in kind is available from a charity or another section of the local authority.

Conclusion

In the chapter we have argued that the controllers of resources, local councillors, have had very little impact on decision making on financial aid through social work. They have had neither the confidence nor the interest in the area necessary to make their presence felt. Consequently, the major impetus has been left to the providers of service, the social workers. It is important to stress that the providers of service have not had to wrest the initiative away from the controllers: rather the controllers have left a policy vacuum which the providers have had to fill.

In this situation there are a variety of subsequent possible permutations. We have outlined some though no doubt many others could be suggested. We have also argued that in some instances, although decision making may be left to the providers of services, the determiners of demand and the other agencies in contact can have a role to play. In an attempt to highlight the situations in which this role is likely to be most influential we would suggest that two approaches to decision making be recognized. One is when the main burden of decision making on financial aid is taken by senior social work personnel (headquarters and senior area staff); the other is when the main burden of decision making on financial aid is assumed by or delegated to more junior social work staff. Such a distinction represents extremes and in practice tendencies in one direction will be all that can be isolated; we also recognize that overlaps and interaction occur. Nevertheless, such a distinction will be useful in helping to show how and when the influence of the determiners of demand and the other agencies in contact is most likely to be felt.

As a broad generalization it is hypothesized that the more extensive the influence of senior personnel the more likely it is that the issues considered will involve broad matters of principle, whereas the more extensive the influence of junior personnel the more likely it is that decisions will be based on immediate pressure considerations, pressure exerted by determiners of demand or agencies in contact. The belief underlying this hypothesis is simply that it is easier for senior personnel to ignore day to day pressures because they are not closely subject to them. Clearly they are not isolated completely from such pressures (some senior personnel carry a small caseload and pressure can always be transmitted through more junior staff) but they are more isolated than their junior colleagues. Basic grade social workers are subject to continuing day to day pressures and research has shown that in such circumstances planning and general decisions of principle tend to be ignored.[14]

Senior social work personnel are subject to a variety of pressures: pressures from some councillors to make the service responsive to public demand, pressure from others (sometimes maybe the same ones) to reduce expenditure. We believe that in the case of financial aid senior personnel are likely to take decisions to restrict aid to certain categories of client and are likely to lay down rules to prevent pressure from clients or other agencies in contact leading to increased payments in what they consider to be unsuitable circumstances.

We have noted a number of the pressures that seem to be brought to bear on basic grade social workers in the area of financial aid. For example, we have referred to the pressures from clients who suffer economic and social deprivation. Our research showed that basic grade social workers feel extremely anxious about having to deal with such problems. Few have had any training on such issues on external or in-service training courses, the professional community offers little guidance and many feel personally ill equipped to deal with questions of financial aid. Although many social workers criticize Supplementary Benefits officials for the way that they administer financial aid, most recognize that at least these officials have some skills in judging applications. In such circumstances

Decision making

social workers may merely react to the pressures and adopt the practice of giving a little help, for 'safety's sake'; some may have an almost pathological fear of making the wrong decision. We have also referred to the pressures resulting from the actions of other agencies in contact. One might refer to the effect of the Supplementary Benefits Commission's dislike of extending the range of discretionary benefits or the effect of the actions of the housing or fuel authorities in changing their method of collecting debts or threatening to suspend service unless a debt is paid. Frequently this pressure may be channelled through the client though the source may be the other agency.

We have not attempted to quantify the number of occasions when decisions are left largely or solely in the hands of basic grade social workers or when they assume such responsibility; the nature of our research does not allow us to make global statements with precision. However, we are able to say that of the departments we looked at only a few appeared to have a decision making structure approaching that where the senior personnel take all effective decisions while many more closely approximated to the situation where basic grade social workers took all effective decisions.

Chapter eight

Conclusions

Heywood and Allen undertook their study of financial aid and social work in the latter part of the 1960s. They started their study 'because there was a good deal of concern and confusion in children's departments about the giving of financial aid'. They argued that this concern was natural because although Section 1 of the 1963 Act set limitations and the Home Office memorandum offered guidance, 'many social workers and social administrators had no previous experience or theory to guide them about disbursing money'.[1]

Nearly a decade has elapsed since that statement, yet in many ways, the feelings expressed are just as appropriate today. There is still considerable concern and confusion amongst social workers about giving financial aid and although there is more experience to draw upon, there is little in the way of theory or agreed principles to provide a guide.

When Heywood and Allen wrote their book there was already considerable concern about the way that financial aid had contributed to a blurring of the boundaries between social work and other public agencies, principally the Supplementary Benefits Commission, the fuel and the housing authorities. They noted considerable confusion, for example, about the main areas of discretion of the SBC and the children's departments. One instance they referred to might be quoted:[2]

> When a family supervised by the children's department and receiving supplementary benefit gets into electricity or rent arrears, it is likely that the children's department will feel that this is clearly a case where the SB officers should pay an exceptional needs grant. However, the SB officers have to decide within their own frame of reference whether or not this is an exceptional need, and whether steps can be taken to

prevent it recurring. Complications may arise for them where full benefits have been paid which are supposed to cover fuel and lighting, as well as other necessities. This means that SB officers would, in effect, have to justify paying the bill twice. They must also consider whether their action would discourage the client from saving to pay future bills and encourage him to be less careful with electricity in the expectation that the next bill would be paid.

Boundary problems between the Supplementary Benefits Commission and social service and social work departments are complicated by one further factor: the ignorance and lack of understanding on both sides. Social work and the Supplementary Benefits Commission have different goals, different functions, and the staff are trained on different bases. As a result, there is a great deal of confusion about what discretion each agency holds and how it is exercised.

The boundary problems between social service and social work departments and these other public agencies, if anything, have increased in recent years. We have suggested that a great deal of financial aid through social work has been used to deal with income maintenance problems. We have also noted Jordan's argument[3] that this has happened because social service and social work departments have been forced to take on part of the work of the Supplementary Benefits Commission: as the SBC has centralized its organization and withdrawn many of its emergency services, so social service and social work departments have been forced to take over responsibility for emergency payments.

It would be impossible to assess Jordan's argument fully without a thorough examination of the SBC, its history and its organization. However, we would suggest that while Jordan's argument may have some validity it is difficult to explain recent developments relating to financial aid through social work solely in this way. While it is important to understand why social service and social work departments have been put under pressure to assume income maintenance functions (and Jordan's argument may help to illuminate this area) it is also important to understand why many social service and social work departments have responded to this pressure. In many cases they have done so because they have had no clear idea about how financial aid should be used themselves and no detailed policy on the matter. In other words, financial aid through social work has been used to deal with income maintenance problems, partly because of the pressure social workers have been put under by other agencies, but also partly because of lack of clarity on their own part about their own functions.

In the past many commentators have argued that the boundary problems between the SBC and social service and social work departments can be overcome by better co-ordination and a better exchange of information. Proposals have been made for joint training courses and periods of experience in both organizations.[4] Such proposals are laudable and may help to promote a better understanding of the other organization's method of working and dominant ethos. However, it is our belief that the problems cannot be solved entirely on such a basis. More radical action, including a clearer definition of areas of responsibility, is needed.

Heywood and Allen did not focus centrally on decision making in their book. However, they did touch on the issue and made a number of important comments. They recognized that most authorities do not have specific guidelines covering the award of financial aid. Nevertheless, they argued that there are certain 'informal factors operating within children's departments which may be just as effectively helpful to the worker as official guide lines'. Four informal factors were highlighted. 'First, there is the supervision and help of the experienced senior staff. Second, there are the periodic reviews which some departments undertake of preventive cases, which familiarise staff with the needs of families and their responses to differentiated help. . . .Third, there is the common denominator test applied by the fact that the children's officer or senior worker assesses cases in the light of the need for committee approval. Fourth, there is the approach of the child care officers, whose training is aimed at examining the family's total situation and its needs, both emotional and environmental.' These factors, Heywood and Allen argued, 'ensure that decisions about financial aid are never made in a vacuum'.[5]

We would accept that in most social service and social work departments specific guidance on financial aid is absent; indeed earlier we argued this ourselves. We would also accept that in some departments informal factors can operate to provide guidelines. However, we would argue that the situation is more varied than Heywood and Allen suggest and that in departments where informal guidelines exist, the account by Heywood and Allen gives too stable and ordered an impression. The informal mechanisms working to create guidelines for social workers are usually more informal than Heywood and Allen suggest. Few of these departments seem to undertake the systematic review of financial aid cases referred to: many simply do not have time. Similarly few regularly present the bulk of financial aid payments for committee approval: in most of these departments only large payments are presented and these account for a small percentage of the total. Again, there is no common approach resulting from the training of social workers: few social workers seem to feel that they have been taught a great deal which can be of use when considering financial aid cases. Where informal guidelines exist they are more frequently the result of negotiation between senior staff and basic grade workers or the 'atmosphere' created on the issue in the department.

In some departments, though, even the type of 'informal' guide-lines just described do not seem to exist. Basic grade social workers may be left to 'exercise their own judgment', effectively unfettered. This kind of situation has something in common with the descriptions of Keith-Lucas.[6] Social workers are left to determine cases themselves without formal or all but the most rudimentary informal guidelines, and do so on individualistic criteria.

There must be some concern about such a position. Variations in provision between one local authority area and another, or between one social work office and another, may be acceptable if they are a reaction to differences in 'need', however defined. If, though, variations are not a reaction to differences in need, but a result of the individualistic criteria of social workers and the absence of any guidelines for the award of aid, then this must cause concern. We have argued that some of the variation in the award of financial aid between local authority areas can be accounted for by reference to social and economic conditions, but by no means all of the variation can be accounted for in this way.

A number of writers have expressed concern about the way financial aid can be used as a weapon to coerce clients to accept unwanted guidance on future behaviour. We have discussed the position in the USA and noted the anxiety expressed about the relationship between social work and social assistance in that system. Joel Handler has argued[7] that similar problems have arisen in Britain as a result of the powers granted under the 1963 and 1968 Acts. We have little doubt that on occasions his view is well founded. However, in the majority of cases such fears must centre on potential rather than current practice. Potentially, financial aid could be used as a weapon to coerce clients to accept additional social work, but if this is to happen on a large scale then financial aid needs to move from the crisis function it currently holds. At the moment, as we have argued, financial aid is used in many authorities as a way of responding to a crisis, often created by another public body. If financial aid were used as a more integral part of social work, in some ways more in the fashion anticipated before the introduction of the 1963 Act, then one might have reason to fear that it could be used in a coercive way.

This does not mean, of course, that financial aid has no effect at all on the client/social worker relationship. The fear has been expressed frequently that if the social worker plays a major role in assessing and granting financial aid this will make it more difficult for him to carry out other social work functions. Such fears seem particularly apposite when financial aid takes the form of a loan rather than a grant and are at their height when the social worker is expected not only to assess and award the loan, but also to supervise its repayment. Research from the probation service[8] has shown how the collection of court fines can so dominate the relationship with clients that other work is impossible. Local authority social workers may not face such extreme problems, but there is an analogy. The client may feel that it is in his best interests to 'hide' his true credit position from the collection agent: if this means that the social worker fails to gain full information on the client's circumstances then it may seriously hamper casework as well as debt collection.

It is also worth while noting that the danger of financial aid being used as a coercive weapon seems to be at its height when aid is given as a loan. Although we have argued that currently financial aid is used as a coercive weapon infrequently, when aid is given as a loan the possibility of such a situation arising is heightened. The social worker, for instance, might be drawn, sometimes unconsciously, into imposing a budgeting pattern on a family to ensure that a loan can be repaid. Visits ostensibly to collect loan debts may be a way of gaining entry to a person's home and may be used to open discussion on more general issues.

Of course, this is not to suggest that loans should never be made to clients. There are a number of circumstances in which it might validly be decided that a loan is preferable to a grant. For example, the award of a loan rather than a grant can help to reduce the 'charity' element in financial aid and help clients to retain self respect. Many social workers have reported that clients prefer loans to grants and offer security for aid given (usually family allowance books) with this in mind. Loans may also be appropriate when financial aid is sought simply because of emergency, created say by the loss of a SBC giro. If this is all that is involved then clearly there is reason to believe that a grant is unwarranted. Again, loans may be appropriate if the client merely requires credit to purchase a large item. For instance, a client may wish to purchase a washing machine or an electric fire but may be unable to meet the 'down payments' necessary for hire purchase. If the social worker feels that the article concerned would be particularly valuable and repayment would present no problem then he might be justified in offering a loan. In such circumstances the social service or social work department is coming close to acting as a 'poor man's bank', extending credit to people with whom commercial institutions refuse to deal. The bank analogy can be seen more clearly when it is recognized that some social service and social work departments operate their own system of credit rating: for example, it is much easier to obtain a loan if you have had one in the past and successfully repaid it.

Nevertheless, there are clearly many occasions when giving financial aid as a loan is inappropriate. This is particularly the case when if aid were given as a loan there would be no realistic possibility of the loan's being repaid. This may increase the anxiety of the client and as a result hinder rather than assist the solution of his problems.

The issue of loans is clearly a difficult one to deal with. The area is extremely sensitive and the balance of judgments may be fine. For this reason, we would argue that the policy adopted by some departments of only giving loans, should be reappraised. While loans may be suitable in many cases, or even in most cases dealt with by some authorities, it is difficult to believe that they should be the rule. It is not difficult to understand, though, why such policies arise. Policy makers may believe that it is one way of guarding against their organization taking on the functions of an assistance agency: social workers may welcome the firm guidance as it relieves them of the responsibility for a difficult area of decision making. However, while such a policy may be understandable it is not desirable. Further, policy makers should reflect that such a policy is rarely firmly adhered to. In this context it is instructive to refer back to the experience of the Charity Organisation Society. They had a clear policy of preferring loans to grants, yet the practical difficulties in implementing such a policy meant that in 1871 aid took the form of loans in only 25 per cent of the cases in which assistance was given.

More generally, we would argue that the whole area of financial aid and social work needs review and amendment. The present position satisfies few. Social workers claim that they are taking on the duties of the Supplementary Benefits Commission, SBC personnel complain that they are unable to discover the criteria by which social workers make decisions on financial aid, clients seem to feel that social workers provide an inadequate and ill-defined service, certainly one that is bereft of the safeguards normally associated with state assistance provisions, and policy makers complain that their original intentions have been altered. In practice many of the difficulties, problems and complaints raised can be traced back to the original decision to allow social workers to offer financial aid in 1963. Of course, it is always easy to criticize with the aid of hindsight and these comments need not be seen as a criticism of the framers of the original legislation. We have previously noted that a great deal of social policy legislation has to be fairly loose because it is innovative and it is difficult to predict future demands and behaviour. It is important to recognize, though, that despite the pressure from social workers' organizations, few seemed to have a clear detailed idea about how financial aid was going to be used when it was first introduced: the problems faced when financial aid was not available were well discussed, but this is very different from a discussion about what form the new powers should take and how they should be used. In this context it is worth remembering the discussion's links with the 'problem family' model, itself an ill-defined concept. Consequently the legislation both in 1963 and 1968 was very general and subsequent memoranda failed to provide detailed guidance.

In any reassessment of the position a number of options seem to be open. First, one might adopt the position suggested by Jordan.[9] He has argued that social work and financial aid should be completely separated. In practice we doubt whether this will ever happen. What is more possible is a return to something like the pre 1963 position and this (as far as financial aid is concerned) may be more what Jordan envisaged anyway. Social workers would not have the general statutory ability to give financial aid, though of course, in individual cases they would no doubt find ways of obtaining financial aid for clients, even if it meant giving money out of their own pockets. Such a policy has an immediate appeal: it should solve the bulk of the boundary problems with other public bodies which have arisen in recent years. It could also lead, as Jordan hopes, to a redefinition of the role of social work (social work could be seen as a service available to groups with a variety of needs, not just the poorer members of the community) and to alterations in the method of operation in departments. Jordan was particularly critical of the effect that financial aid powers have had on managerial hierarchies in social work departments.

Such a development might have the corollary that the Supplementary Benefits Commission might itself assume a more social work oriented approach for part of its work. The SBC, of course, has already made some moves in this direction with the appointment of a permanent social work adviser and special welfare officers, but to date such moves have been relatively tentative. The moves anticipated here would be more substantial and would indicate an acceptance of the need to place more emphasis on what Olive Stevenson has discussed in terms of 'creative' rather than 'proportional' justice.[10]

An alternative is what might be seen as the opposite extreme. Social work might expand its activity in the field of financial aid. The spur to such a development might be provided by the current revision of the Supplementary Benefits Scheme. Social service and social work departments might take over a greater degree of formal responsibility for discretionary payments. In such circumstances the Supplementary Benefits Commission might restrict its activity almost

Conclusions

entirely to the provision of scale benefits; any additional or emergency aid might be provided locally by the social service or social work department.

Such a development might have an appeal to those who would like to see more local variations in assistance payments (to take account of differences in 'need'), to those who believe that social workers are better suited to administer discretionary payments than the SBC, and to those who recognize that an organization like the SBC has to develop rules that might result in aid being refused to needy cases. As an illustration of this latter instance one might refer to a situation where a client has received all his assistance entitlement but has spent it unwisely and consequently is still in need. While an assistance service might find it difficult to formulate rules and instruct staff for such situations, the intervention of a social work agency with the power to assess the position might be acceptable. Support for social work taking over responsibility for discretionary assistance payments might also be forthcoming from those who recognize the value of 'second doors' in the social services on which dissatisfied claimants or clients can knock.

Such a development could well lead to the establishment of specialist branches of social work which would only deal with financial aid. Certainly if social work took on more responsibility for financial aid then the growth in the workload, and the potential impact on other aspects of the service, might persuade many departments to 'hive off' financial aid functions: in this context the Glasgow experiment[11] might provide something of a model. It might also lead local authorities to ask for more central government finance to meet the expansion in their commitments.

Such a development could also be the predecessor of an attempt to integrate more generally social assistance and social work services. This would imply an acceptance of the view that a client's social, psychological and material needs cannot be separated, but must be treated as a whole. We have noted that such an approach has been adopted by many other countries. The American experience has led many to be sceptical of its consequences, but other commentators have pointed out that a number of European countries seem to have avoided some of the worst pitfalls. The integration of social work services and financial services at the local level, as in many European countries, would be welcomed by writers like Lafitte. He argues that 'the balance of advantage' might in the future lie in 'abolishing the S.B.C., denationalising assistance, vesting in social service departments individual responsibility for the residual relief of financial hardship, and reverting (in Marshall's words) to the "ancient tradition of the Western World"—still the current tradition of our European neighbours—"that the relief of the poor was the affair of their neighbours"'.[12]

Interestingly Jordan would not completely rule out moves in such a direction. He states explicitly that there 'could be a case' for basing a residual assistance service (an important part of his argument is that the present assistance service has to deal with too many clients: it is not the kind of residual service Beveridge intended) 'on the local authorities'. Indeed, he goes on, 'the development of the social services departments, and their increasing resemblance to the old Public Assistance Committees, suggests that the best plan might be to use their field work services precisely for this purpose'. However, he stresses that if this were done then 'public provision for personal social services, staffed by professional social workers, and for residential services, would have to be moved to a quite separate local authority department'. For Jordan it 'is the mixture of public assistance and social work that is so fatal to the social worker's professional task, and to the interests of their clients in need of either service' not the level, national or local, at which assistance services are provided.[13]

A further alternative is something of a middle way. Of course, the present position represents something of a middle way, but it might be argued that a more strictly defined and better organized middle way could be found. The reasons why such a strategy might be supported have a great deal in common with the support for the financial aid provisions of the 1963 and 1968 Acts. They would involve a recognition that a national assistance agency is best suited to administer financial aid services, even when discretion is involved, but a belief that without the power to give aid themselves the social workers' task is made more difficult.

However, as has been indicated, if a middle way is to be proposed for the future, then it has to be more tightly defined than in the past. First, decisions need to be made about the kind of areas in which social workers should be involved. A number of alternatives exist: they include what have been termed 'preventive' and 'promotional' work. Preventive work means that social workers would give aid not to meet an immediate crisis but to forestall development of such a situation in the future (in the past it has been expressed as taking action which would avoid greater expense to the local authority in the future); promotional work would allow social workers to take action which would lift clients and groups above contemporary minimum standards (such as the provision of holidays, payment of fees for pre school play groups or music lessons) and to assist in community development.

Once decisions about the areas in which social workers should be given power have been made then they may need to be translated into legislative provisions or at least made the subject of official memoranda. Clearly there will also be the need for relevant pre and in-service training covering such issues and official policy guidance.

Conclusions

It may be, though, that such a prescription will fail at the first hurdle: it may be practically impossible to define tightly the area to be covered by social work. Preventive and promotional social work are terms which have been used increasingly of late, but though it is possible to give examples of the kind of activity covered, it is extremely difficult to define tightly the terms and distinguish between them. In this context it is worth while noting the comments of Leissner who studied preventive services under the 1963 Act. He said: 'Our observations have shown that, in practice the concept of prevention is as loosely and widely, or as narrowly applied as the individual worker deems fit'.[14] It is also worth while commenting that the areas described by these terms are very similar to those described by people before the 1963 Act. At that time it proved impossible to define the areas tightly enough; this may still prove to be too big a task.

More generally, a middle way in financial aid, if it is to be effective, can only operate in a structure of social services in which social work itself has a clearly defined role, in which social workers have a clear 'raison d'être' and in which social workers have established methods of practice. If social work cannot live up to these prescriptions then a middle way is bound to present problems. It will be difficult to define tightly the way in which social workers should use financial aid if one cannot say at the outset how social workers undertake their task, and if the way in which social workers should use financial aid cannot be defined tightly then boundary problems inevitably will arise. In our introduction we said that the problems over financial aid mirrored those of social work in general. In our conclusion we would argue that if the problems facing social work in general are not solved, or if, as some would argue, they are not amenable to solution, or even if their solution is undesirable, then an effective middle way with financial aid may be impossible.

Finally, what if no effective major reappraisal takes place? In such an eventuality it seems likely that gradually more social work departments will withdraw from the major part of present financial aid activity. The pressure will come from a number of different sources: from social workers who feel that they are being forced to take over the job of the Supplementary Benefits Commission and from local authority councillors who are looking more carefully at any area of expenditure that can be reduced. Such pressures may mean that senior staff will be forced to lay down rules about financial aid, but because it is so difficult to lay down positive rules, specifying how aid should be used (and to enforce them), the rules will be negative. They will, for example, severely restrict the groups of clients who can be helped with financial aid, and the reasons for which help can be given. Trends in this direction can already be seen.

118

Some authorities, of course, may resist such trends, while others may develop new ways of using financial aid. It appears, though, as if the majority will follow the road described above and will withdraw to a minimum use of financial aid. It has been suggested to us that such a position might have some benefits; that if little financial aid is available social workers will be forced to think more carefully about each individual case and will have to justify their use of financial aid to their colleagues and themselves. However, in the absence of a clearer view about the positive ways in which financial aid should be used and a clearer measure against which individual cases can be judged we doubt whether the result will be anything like the framers and pursuers of the 1963 and 1968 Acts had in mind.

Notes

Introduction

1 Local Authority Social Services Act 1970. Provisions introduced in 1971.
2 Social Work (Scotland) Act 1968. Provisions introduced in 1969.
3 In England this centred on the Seebohm Report, *Report of the Committee on Local Authority and Allied Personal Social Services*, HMSO, London, 1968, Cmnd 3703.
4 Previously social work had been carried out in a variety of different local authority departments. It was widely believed that this resulted in lack of co-ordination and unhelpful overlap in provision of service.
5 The National Institute for Social Work research unit have undertaken an evaluation of developments in Hampshire. See J. E. Neill, D. Fruin, E. M. Goldberg and R. W. Warburton, 'Reactions to integration', *Social Work Today,* vol. 4, no. 15, pp. 458-65, and A. McKay, E. M. Goldberg and D. Fruin, 'Consumers and a social service department', *Social Work Today*, vol. 4, no. 16, 1973, pp. 486-91.
6 Z. T. Butrym, *The Nature of Social Work*, Macmillan, London, 1976, p. 134. Brill describes the period before 1970 as one in which the definition of social work functions was given much attention. See M. Brill, 'The local authority social worker', in K. Jones (ed.), *The Year Book of Social Policy 1971*, Routledge & Kegan Paul, London, 1972, p. 81.
7 N. Timms, *Social Casework: Principles and Practice*, Routledge & Kegan Paul, London, 1964, p. 8.

Chapter 1   Britain: post Second World War experience

1 An exception was the War Pensioners' welfare service.
2 Discretionary allowances received only passing mention in the Beveridge Report and no guidance was given in the National Assistance Act 1948. They were dealt with entirely by regulations.

3 Assistance could be granted where earnings were exceptionally low because of disablement. The Family Allowances Act 1946 introduced benefits for all families with two or more children, but there was no equivalent to the discretionary allowance of National Assistance for 'working families'.

4 M. Rooff, *A Hundred Years of Family Welfare*, Michael Joseph, London, 1972, p. 178.

5 However, voluntary organizations remained significant. The 1951 Census gave 6,086 social welfare workers in non government employment, compared with 4,169 in national and local government service. See R. G. Walton, *Women in Social Work*, Routledge & Kegan Paul, London, 1975, p. 200. Jeffreys records information on eight voluntary casework agencies in Buckinghamshire in 1961-2. Referrals were mostly from the NAB and local authority health and welfare departments (though nearly half the clients were self referred). Most clients were referred for financial assistance, though the range of problems dealt with and services given was much wider. M. Jeffreys, *An Anatomy of Social Welfare Services*, Michael Joseph, London, 1965, pp. 266, 273. See also *Report of the Committee on One-Parent Families*, HMSO, London, 1974, Cmnd 5629, para. 8.90.

6 D. V. Donnison, *The Ingleby Report: Three Critical Essays*, Fabian Society, London, 1962, p. 2.

7 J. Packman, *The Child's Generation: Child Care Policy from Curtis to Houghton*, Basil Blackwell and Martin Robertson, London, 1975, p. 32.

8 K. McDougal, 'Social work in the Health Service', in W. A. J. Farndale (ed.), *Trends in the National Health Service*, Pergamon Press, London, 1964, p. 109.

9 Some local authorities, with the approval of the Ministry of Health, used Section 28 of the National Health Service Act 1946 to give material assistance to prevent illness or provide care or after care. They could levy a charge according to the recipient's means. A few authorities used this power to provide such things as beds and cooking utensils. See *Report of the Committee on Children and Young Persons* (Ingleby Report), HMSO, London, 1960, Cmnd 1191, para. 24.

10 An indication that fuel costs became an increasing problem is that NAB discretionary allowances (see note 12) for additional fuel rose from 2·6 per cent of the total in 1948 to 13·6 per cent in 1956 and 30·3 per cent in 1965. See V. N. George, *Social Security: Beveridge and After*, Routledge & Kegan Paul, London, 1968, p. 220.

11 Hospital social workers, transferred from the NHS to local authorities in 1976, could call on charitable funds donated to their hospitals.

12 These were additions to weekly payments. Individuals could receive more than one addition each week. Exceptional needs grants, which were for single items of special expenditure, such as replacement of bedding, increased more slowly from 101,500 in 1949 to 178,000 in 1959. See George, op. cit., pp. 221-2.

Notes

13 Jeffreys, op. cit., p. 113.
14 See for example M. L. Ferard and N. K. Hunnybun, *The Caseworker's Use of Relationships*, Tavistock Publications, London, 1962.
15 See E. Heimler, 'The Hendon Experiment', *Mental Illness and Social Work*, Penguin, Harmondsworth, 1967, chapter 7, pp. 106-29.
16 See P. Townsend, 'Area deprivation policies', *New Statesman*, 6 August 1976, pp. 168-71.
17 *Report of the Working Party on Social Workers in the Local Authority Health and Welfare Services* (Younghusband Report) HMSO, London, 1959, para. 316.
18 For a review of the literature see A. F. Philp and N. Timms, *The Problem of 'The Problem Family'*, Family Service Units, London, 1962.
19 'New light on an old problem', *The Times Weekly Review*, 11 November 1954, quoted by Philp and Timms, op. cit., p. 39.
20 See for example F. M. G. Willson, 'The administrative consequences of Jim and Vera Fardell', *Administrators in Action*, Allen & Unwin, London, 1961, pp. 279-350.
21 See A. F. Philp, *Family Failure: A study of 129 families with multiple problems*, Faber, London, 1963.
22 In evidence, *Report of the Committee on Local Authority and Allied Personal Social Services*, HMSO, London, 1968, Cmnd 3703, quoted by A. Leissner, *Family Advice Services*, Humanities Press, New York, 1967, p. 36.
23 See Packman, op. cit., chapter 4, 'An even better and cheaper way', pp. 52-74.
24 See ibid., pp. 53-4.
25 Ibid., p. 56.
26 Ibid., p. 59.
27 Ibid., p. 60.
28 R. T. Easton, 'Preventive casework in children's departments', *Case Conference*, vol. 5, no. 8, February 1959, pp. 211-13.
29 See Donnison, op. cit., p. 5.
30 *Report of the Committee on Children and Young Persons*, HMSO, London, 1960, Cmnd 1191, para. 8.
31 Scots Law defined parental neglect under Section 12 (2) of the Children and Young Persons Act 1937 as neglecting a child or young person 'in a manner likely to cause injury to his health (by failing to provide) adequate food, clothing, medical aid or lodging'.
32 *Report of the Committee on Children and Young Persons*, para. 39.
33 Ibid., para. 46.

Chapter 2 Britain: developments since Ingleby

1 Children and Young Persons Act 1963, Section 1.
2 *Hansard*, vol. 672, 1963, col. 1270.
3 *Home Office Circular 204*, 1963.

4 Ibid., para. 13.
5 Ibid., appendix para. 3.
6 Quoted in R. Lister and T. Emmett, *Under the Safety Net*, Child Poverty Action Group, London, 1976.
7 J. S. Heywood and B. K. Allen, *Financial Help in Social Work*, Manchester University Press, 1971.
8 K. Carmichael, 'The relationship between social work departments and the DHSS: the use of the Social Work (Scotland) Act, Section 12', in *In Cash or Kind*, papers delivered at a conference held in the Department of Social Administration, University of Edinburgh, November 1974.
9 Health Services and Public Health Act 1968, Section 45.
10 Ibid., Section 45.
11 M. Hawker and T. Emmett, *Survey in the London Boroughs of Section 1, Children and Young Persons Act 1963 Payments*, British Association of Social Workers Poverty Group, London, 1974.
12 S. Ross, 'A study of the use of cash payments made under Section 1 of the Children and Young Persons Act, 1963', unpublished dissertation, University of York, 1975.
13 Report of the Committee of the Scottish Advisory Council on Children, *Prevention of Neglect of Children*, HMSO, Edinburgh, 1962, Cmnd 1966.
14 Scottish Home and Health Department, *Social Work and the Community*, HMSO, Edinburgh, 1966, Cmnd 3065.
15 Social Work (Scotland) Act 1968, Section 12.
16 Carmichael, op. cit., p. 54.
17 Social Work (Scotland) Act 1968, Section 12.

Chapter 3 Relationships between social work and other public agencies

1 *Social Insurance and Allied Services*, HMSO, London, 1942, Cmd 6404.
2 A number of studies have shown the way in which officials build up their own system of informal rules which sometimes conflict with official guidelines. For example, see P. M. Blau, *The Dynamics of Bureaucracy*, University of Chicago Press, 1963.
3 The number of exceptional circumstances payments decreased until the early 1970s although much of this decrease was a result of transitionary arrangements.
4 Department of Health and Social Security, Supplementary Benefits Commission, *Exceptional Needs Payments*, HMSO, London, 1973.
5 Letter dated 6 January 1975.
6 This accounts for the relatively few discretionary payments made to cover items such as rent.
7 Home Office Circular 204, 1963.
8 B. Jordan, 'Emergency payments: a social security responsibility', *Social Work Today*, vol. 3, no. 23, 1973.
9 Ibid., p. 15.

Notes

10 Social Work Services Group, *Joint Memorandum of Guidance: Fuel Debts in Scotland*, Scottish Education Department, Edinburgh, 1973.
11 D. Donnison, 'Against discretion', *New Society*, 15 September 1977, pp. 534-6.
12 Ibid., p. 536.
13 O. Stevenson, *Claimant or Client?*, Allen & Unwin, London, 1973.
14 B. Jordan, 'Against Donnison', *New Society*, 13 October 1977, pp. 69-70.
15 R. Lister and T. Emmett, *Under the Safety Net*, Child Poverty Action Group, London, 1976, p. 25.
16 B. Gearing and G. Sharp, *Exceptional Needs Payments and the Elderly*, Community Development Project Occasional Paper, Coventry, 1973.
17 See, for example, D. Marsden, *Mothers Alone*, Routledge & Kegan Paul, London, 1968.
18 The exceptional circumstances payments increasingly have been used to cover heating costs, though they are by no means an automatic allowance.
19 Letter to BASW, Social Policy and Action Group, August 1974.
20 B. Jordan, *Poor Parents*, Routledge & Kegan Paul, London, 1974.
21 See also unpublished papers, available on application from the authors.
22 A measure used until 1973 to prevent social assistance payments exceeding a previous wage.
23 *Report of the Committee on One-Parent Families*, HMSO, London, 1974, Cmnd 5629.
24 Originally highlighted in the Beveridge Report.
25 J. Heywood and B. Allen, *Financial Help in Social Work*, Manchester University Press, 1971.
26 Report prepared by London Borough of Tower Hamlets, Social Services Department.
27 M. Hawker and T. Emmett, *Survey in the London Boroughs of Section 1, Children and Young Persons Act 1963 Payments*, British Association of Social Workers Poverty Group, London, 1974.
28 Figures produced by individual unpublished surveys.
29 See, for example, letter in reply to Jordan's *New Society* article, *New Society*, 27 October 1977.
30 British Association of Social Workers, Scottish Region, letter to Social Work Departments and Supplementary Benefits Commission, dated 28 October 1974.
31 Issued by Scottish Region of BASW, 30 October 1974.
32 Quoted by Jordan, 1973, op. cit.
33 London Borough of Tower Hamlets, op. cit.
34 Hawker and Emmett, op. cit.
35 Report of the Sub-Committee to the Scottish Housing Advisory Committee, *Housing Management*, HMSO, Edinburgh, 1967, para. 82.
36 See for example, W. B. Herbert, 'Who owes rent?', *Sociological Review*, vol. 13, 1965, pp. 149-56.

37 Report of Sub-Committee to the Scottish Housing Advisory
    Committee, op. cit.
38 See Social Work Services Group, op. cit.

Chapter 4   Social work and assistance services: comparative experience

1   O. Stevenson, *Claimant or Client?*, Allen & Unwin, London, 1973.
2   L. Komisar, *Down and Out in the USA*, New Viewpoints, New
    York, 1974, pp. 14-15.
3   W. Bell, *Aid to Dependent Children*, Columbia University Press,
    New York, 1965.
4   Ibid., p. 146.
5   Komisar, op. cit., pp. 75-6.
6   W. Bell, 'Too few services to separate', *Social Work*, vol. 18, no. 2,
    1973, p. 67.
7   A. Keith-Lucas, *Decisions about People's Need: A Study of
    Administrative Responses in Public Assistance*, University of North
    Carolina, 1957, p. 34.
8   Ibid., p. 245.
9   Ibid., p. 35.
10 P. L. Bushey, 'Public assistance agencies—social work practice',
    Encyclopedia of Social Work, National Association of Social
    Workers, New York, 1965, pp. 600-5.
11 A. Kadushin, *Child Welfare Services*, Macmillan, New York, 1967,
    p. 143.
12 Ibid.
13 Ibid., p. 157
14 J. Handler and E. J. Hollingsworth, *The Deserving Poor: A Study of
    Welfare Administration*, Academic Press, New York, 1971, p. 201.
15 Ibid., p. 202.
16 See I. Piliavin and A. E. Gross, 'The effects of separation of services
    and income maintenance on AFDC recipients', *Social Service
    Review*, vol. 51, no. 3, 1977, pp. 389-406.
17 Bell, op. cit., 1973, p. 72.
18 Stevenson, op. cit., p. 29.

Chapter 5   Social work practice and financial aid

1   M. Rooff, *A Hundred Years of Family Welfare*, Michael Joseph,
    London, 1972, p. 320.
2   Ibid., p. 327.
3   M. E. Richmond, *Social Diagnosis*, Collier-Macmillan, New York,
    1965, first published 1917. Richmond planned a volume on 'social
    treatment' but never completed it.
4   Rooff, op. cit., p. 336.
5   See pp. 74-5.
6   Rooff, op. cit., p. 332.
7   See pp. 71-2.
8   G. Hamilton, *Theory and Practice of Social Casework*, Columbia
    University Press, New York, 1951.

Notes

9 H. H. Perlman, *Social Casework: A Problem Solving Process*, University of Chicago Press, 1957.
10 F. Hollis, *Casework: A Psychosocial Therapy*, Random House, New York, 1972.
11 N. Timms, *Social Casework: Principles and Practice*, Routledge & Kegan Paul, London, 1964.
12 D. Jehu, *Learning Theory and Social Work*, Routledge & Kegan Paul, London, 1967.
13 A. Pincus and A. Minahan, *Social Work Practice: Model and Method*, Peacock, Itasco, Illinois, 1973.
14 J. E. Mayer and N. Timms, *The Client Speaks: Working Class Impressions of Casework*, Routledge & Kegan Paul, London, 1970.
15 Hamilton, op. cit., p. 6.
16 Ibid., p. 91.
17 Ibid., p. 92.
18 Hollis, op. cit., p. 81.
19 Ibid., p. 26.
20 Ibid., p. 26.
21 Perlman, op. cit., pp. 32-3.
22 Ibid., p. 34.
23 Ibid., p. 60.
24 Timms, op. cit., p. 198.
25 Mayer and Timms, op. cit.
26 Jehu, op. cit., p. 117.
27 Ibid., p. 97.
28 Ibid., p. 108.
29 Pincus and Minnahan, op. cit., p. 3.
30 Ibid., p. 19.
31 Ibid., p. 31.
32 B. Jordan, *Poor Parents*, Routledge & Kegan Paul, London, 1974, p. 99.
33 Ibid., p. 110.
34 Ibid., p. 102.
35 J. Handler, *The Coercive Social Worker: British Lessons for American Social Services*, Rand McNally, Chicago, 1973.

Chapter 6   Variations in the provision of financial aid

1 In Britain this interest is best reflected by Bledwyn Davies and colleagues: see for example, B. P. Davies *et al.*, *Variations in Services for the Aged*, Bell, London, 1971. See also J. Packman, *Child Care, Needs and Numbers*, Allen & Unwin, London, 1968; N. Boaden, *Urban Policy Making*, Cambridge University Press, 1971.
2 See, for example, S. Holtemann, 'Areas of urban deprivation in Great Britain: an analysis of 1971 Census data', *Social Trends*, vol. 6, 1975, pp. 33-47.
3 See B. P. Davies *et al.*, *Social Needs and Resources in Local Services*, Michael Joseph, London, 1968.

4 *Home Office Circular 204*, 1963.
5 See H. L. Willensky and C. N. Lebaux, *Industrial Society and Social Welfare*, Free Press, New York, 1965.
6 B. P. Davies *et al.*, op. cit.
7 F. Williams, 'Cash Assistance for Families', unpublished, quoted by R. Lister and T. Emmett, *Under the Safety Net*, Child Poverty Action Group, London, 1976.
8 Current studies include those by M. Hill, now at the University of Bristol.
9 For further details, application should be made to the authors.

Chapter 7 Decision making

1 The differences between public and private administration are a source of major controversy. The Brunel Social Services Organization Research Unit has been particularly influential in Britain in applying techniques developed from a study of private enterprise to the social services. See R. Rowbottam, A. Hay, D. Bills, *Social Services Departments*, Heinemann, London, 1974, for an example of their work.
2 See, for example, D. Marsden, *Mothers Alone*, Routledge & Kegan Paul, London, 1968.
3 D. V. Donnison, V. Chapman *et al.*, *Social Policy and Administration*, Allen & Unwin, London, 1965.
4 Ibid., p. 234.
5 P. M. Blau, *The Dynamics of Bureaucracy*, University of Chicago Press, 1963.
6 K. Carmichael, 'The relationship between social work departments and the DHSS: the use of the Social Work (Scotland) Act, Section 12', in *In Cash or Kind*, papers delivered at a conference held in the Department of Social Administration, University of Edinburgh, November 1974.
7 J. Handler, *The Coercive Social Worker: British Lessons for American Social Services*, Rand McNally, Chicago, 1973.
8 L. Moss and S. R. Parker, *The Local Government Councillor*, HMSO, London, 1967.
9 D. Middleton, 'A cash code for social workers', paper prepared for British Association of Social Workers (Scotland), 31 March 1976. See also *Social Work Today*, vol. 9, no. 8, 1977, pp. 16-17, which the reports decision of the Council of British Association of Social Workers.
10 See, for example, B. Glastonbury, M. Burdett and R. Austin, 'Community perceptions and the personal social services', *Policy and Politics*, vol. 1, no. 3, March 1973, pp. 191-211; A. Glampson, B. Glastonbury and D. Fruin, 'Knowledge and perceptions of the social services', *Journal of Social Policy*, vol. 6, no. 1, 1977, pp. 1-16; U. Maclean, 'Sources of help', *New Society*, 5 April 1973, pp. 16-17.
11 Possibly the best examples come from studies of the National Health Service, though examples can be gained from the range of services introduced after 1945.

Notes

12 In this context one might refer to the individualistic theories
    associated with the psychoanalytic school.
13 Handler, op. cit.
14 See, for example, R. G. S. Brown, *The Administrative Process in
    Britain*, Methuen, London, 1970.

Chapter 8 Conclusions

1   J. S. Heywood and B. K. Allen, *Financial Help in Social Work*,
    Manchester University Press, 1971, p. 70.
2   Ibid., p. 18.
3   B. Jordan, *Poor Parents*, Routledge & Kegan Paul, London, 1974.
4   O. Stevenson, *Claimant or Client?*, Allen & Unwin, London, 1973.
5   Heywood and Allen, op. cit., pp. 14-15.
6   A. Keith-Lucas, *Decisions About People's Needs: A Study of
    Administrative Responses in Public Assistance*, University of North
    Carolina, 1957.
7   J. Handler, *The Coercive Social Worker: British Lessons for
    American Social Services*, Rand McNally, Chicago, 1973.
8   M. Davies, *Financial Penalties and Probation*, Home Office
    Research Unit, HMSO, London, 1970.
9   Jordan, op. cit.
10 Stevenson, op. cit.
11 See p. 45-6.
12 F. Lafitte, 'The relief function', in M. J. Brown (ed.), *Social Issues
    and the Social Services*, Charles Knight, London, 1974, pp. 235-6.
13 Jordan, op. cit., pp. 180-1.
14 A. Leissner, *Family Advice Services*, Humanities Press, New York,
    1967, p. 36.

Bibliography

Bell, W., *Aid to Dependent Children*, Columbia University Press, New York, 1965.

Bell, W., 'Too few services to separate', *Social Work*, vol. 18, no. 2, 1973.

Blau, P. M., *The Dynamics of Bureaucracy*, University of Chicago Press, 1963.

Boaden, N., *Urban Policy Making*, Cambridge University Press, 1971.

Brill, M., 'The local authority social worker', in K. Jones (ed.), *The Year Book of Social Policy 1971*, Routledge & Kegan Paul, London, 1972.

Brown, M. J. (ed.), *Social Issues and the Social Services*, Charles Knight, London, 1974.

Brown, R. G. S., *The Administrative Process in Britain*, Methuen, London, 1970.

Bushey, P. L., 'Public assistance agencies-social work practice', *Encyclopedia of Social Work*, National Association of Social Workers, New York, 1965, pp. 600-5.

Butrym, Z. T., *The Nature of Social Work*, Macmillan, London, 1976.

Carmichael, K., 'The relationship between social work departments and the DHSS: the use of the Social Work (Scotland) Act, Section 12', in *In Cash or Kind*, papers delivered at a conference held in the Department of Social Administration, University of Edinburgh, November 1974.

Davies, B. P. *et al.*, *Social Needs and Resources in Local Services*, Michael Joseph, London, 1968.

Davies, B. P. *et al.*, *Variations in Services for the Aged*, Bell, London, 1971.

Davies, M., *Financial Penalties and Probation*, Home Office Research Unit, HMSO, London, 1970.

Department of Health and Social Security, Supplementary Benefits Commission, *Exceptional Needs Payments*, HMSO, London, 1973.

Donnison, D., *The Ingleby Report: Three Critical Essays*, Fabian Society, London, 1962.

Donnison, D., 'Against discretion', *New Society*, 15 September 1977, pp. 534-6.

Bibliography

Donnison, D. V., Chapman, V. *et al.*, *Social Policy and Administration*, Allen & Unwin, London, 1965.

Easton, R. T., 'Preventive casework in children's departments', *Case Conference*, vol. 5, no. 8, February 1959, pp. 211-13.

Farndale, W. A. J. (ed.), *Trends in the National Health Service*, Pergamon Press, London, 1964.

Ferard, M. L. and Hunnybun, N. K., *The Caseworker's Use of Relationships*, Tavistock Publications, London, 1962.

Gearing, B. and Sharp, G., *Exceptional Needs Payments and the Elderly*, Community Development Project Occasional Paper, Coventry, 1973.

George, V. N., *Social Security: Beveridge and After*, Routledge & Kegan Paul, London, 1968.

Glampson, A., Glastonbury, B. and Fruin, D., 'Knowledge and perceptions of the social services', *Journal of Social Policy*, vol. 6, no. 1, 1977, pp. 1-16.

Glastonbury, B., Burdett, M. and Austin, R., 'Community perceptions and the personal social services', *Policy and Politics*, vol. 1, no. 3, March 1973, pp. 191-211.

Hamilton, G., *Theory and Practice of Social Casework*, Columbia University Press, New York, 1951.

Handler, J., *The Coercive Social Worker: British Lessons for American Social Services*, Rand McNally, Chicago, 1973.

Handler, J. and Hollingsworth, E. J., *The Deserving Poor: A Study of Welfare Administration*, Academic Press, New York, 1971.

Hawker, M. and Emmett, T., *Survey in the London Boroughs of Section 1, Children and Young Persons Act 1963 Payments*, British Association of Social Workers Poverty Group, London, 1974.

Heimler, E., *Mental Illness and Social Work*, Penguin, Harmondsworth, 1967.

Herbert, W. B., 'Who owes rent?' *Sociological Review*, vol. 13, 1965, pp. 149-56.

Heywood, J. S. and Allen, B. K., *Financial Help in Social Work*, Manchester University Press, 1971.

Hollis, F., *Casework: A Psychosocial Therapy*, Random House, New York, 1972.

Holtemann, S., 'Areas of urban deprivation in Great Britain: an analysis of 1971 Census data', *Social Trends*, vol. 6, 1975, pp. 33-47.

Jeffreys, M., *An Anatomy of Social Welfare Services*, Michael Joseph, London, 1965.

Jehu, D., *Learning Theory and Social Work*, Routledge & Kegan Paul, London, 1967.

Jones, K. (ed.), *The Year Book of Social Policy 1971*, Routledge & Kegan Paul, London, 1972.

Jordan, B., 'Emergency payments: a social security responsibility', *Social Work Today*, vol. 3, no. 23, 1973, pp. 15-16.

Jordan, B., *Poor Parents*, Routledge & Kegan Paul, London, 1974.

Jordan, B., 'Against Donnison', *New Society*, 13 October 1977, pp. 69-70.

Kadushin, A., *Child Welfare Services*, Macmillan, New York, 1967.

Keith-Lucas, A., *Decisions About People's Need: A Study of Administrative Responses in Public Assistance*, University of North Carolina, 1957.

Komisar, L., *Down and Out in the USA*, New Viewpoints, New York, 1974.

Lafitte, F., 'The relief function', in M. J. Brown (ed.), *Social Issues and the Social Services*, Charles Knight, London, 1974.

Leissner, A., *Family Advice Services*, Humanities Press, New York, 1967.

Lister, R. and Emmett, T., *Under the Safety Net*, Child Poverty Action Group, London, 1976.

McDougal, K., 'Social work in the Health Service', in W. A. J. Farndale (ed.), *Trends in the National Health Service*, Pergamon Press, London, 1964.

McKay, A., Goldberg, E. M. and Fruin, D., 'Consumers and a social service department', *Social Work Today*, vol. 4, no. 16, 1973, pp. 486-91.

McLean, U., 'Sources of help', *New Society*, 5 April 1973, pp. 16-17.

Marsden, D., *Mothers Alone*, Routledge & Kegan Paul, London, 1968.

Mayer, J. E. and Timms, N., *The Client Speaks: Working Class Impressions of Casework*, Routledge & Kegan Paul, London, 1970.

Moss, L. and Parker, S. R., *The Local Government Councillor*, HMSO, London, 1967.

Neill, J. E., Fruin, D., Goldberg, E. M. and Warburton, R. W., 'Reactions to integration', *Social Work Today*, vol. 4, no. 15, 1973, pp. 458-65.

Packman, J., *Child Care, Needs and Numbers*, Allen & Unwin, London, 1968.

Packman, J., *The Child's Generation: Child Care Policy from Curtis to Houghton*, Basil Blackwell and Martin Robertson, London, 1975.

Perlman, H. H., *Social Casework: A Problem Solving Process*, University of Chicago Press, 1957.

Philp, A. F., *Family Failure: A Study of 129 Families with Multiple Problems*, Faber, London, 1963.

Philp, A. F. and Timms, N., *The Problem of the 'Problem Family'*, Family Service Units, London, 1962.

Piliavin, I. and Gross, A. E., 'The effects of separation of services and income maintenance on AFDC recipients', *Social Service Review*, vol. 51, no. 3, 1977, pp. 389-406.

Pincus, A. and Minahan, A., *Social Work Practice: Model and Method*, Peacock, Itasco, Illinois, 1973.

Report of the Committee on Local Authority and Allied Personal Social Services, HMSO, London, 1968, Cmnd 3703.

Report of the Committee on Children and Young Persons, HMSO, London, 1960, Cmnd 1191.

Report of the Committee on One-Parent Families, HMSO, London, 1974, Cmnd 5629.

Report of the Working Party on Social Workers in the Local Authority Health and Welfare Services, HMSO, London, 1959.

Bibliography

Richmond, M. E., *Social Diagnosis*, Collier-Macmillan, New York, 1965.

Rooff, M., *A Hundred Years of Family Welfare*, Michael Joseph, London, 1972.

Rowbottam, R., Hay, A. and Bills, D., *Social Services Departments*, Heinemann, London, 1974.

Scottish Advisory Council on Children, *Prevention of Neglect of Children*, HMSO, Edinburgh, 1962, Cmnd 1966.

Scottish Education Department, *Social Work in Scotland 1969*, HMSO, Edinburgh, 1970, Cmnd 4475.

Scottish Home and Health Department, *Social Work and the Community*, HMSO, Edinburgh, 1966, Cmnd 3065.

Scottish Home and Health Department, *Housing Management*, HMSO, Edinburgh, 1967.

Social Insurance and Allied Services, HMSO, London, 1942, Cmd 6404.

Social Work Services Group, *Joint Memorandum of Guidance: Fuel Debts in Scotland*, Scottish Education Department, Edinburgh, 1973.

Stevenson, O., *Claimant or Client?*, Allen & Unwin, London, 1973.

Timms, N., *Social Casework: Principles and Practice*, Routledge & Kegan Paul, London, 1964.

Townsend, P., 'Area deprivation policies', *New Statesman*, 6 August 1976, pp. 168-71.

Walton, R. G., *Women in Social Work*, Routledge & Kegan Paul, London, 1975.

Willensky, H. L. and Lebaux, C. N., *Industrial Society and Social Welfare*, Free Press, New York, 1965.

Willson, F. M. G., *Administrators in Action*, Allen & Unwin, London, 1961.

Index

Index

For Product Safety Concerns and Information please contact our EU
representative GPSR@taylorandfrancis.com
Taylor & Francis Verlag GmbH, Kaufingerstraße 24, 80331 München, Germany